CW00708962

AGENDA FOR GROWTH

by Andrea Westall and
Marc Cowling

INSTITUTE FOR PUBLIC POLICY RESEARCH

INSTITUTE FOR PUBLIC POLICY RESEARCH

30-32 Southampton St
London WC2E 7RA
Tel: 0171 470 6100
Fax: 0171 470 6111
postmaster@ippr.org.uk
www.ippr.org.uk
Registered charity 800065

The Institute for Public Policy Research is an independent charity whose purpose is to contribute to public understanding of social, economic and political questions through research, discussion and publication. It was established in 1988 by leading figures in the academic, business and trade-union communities to provide an alternative to the free market think tanks.

IPPR's research agenda reflects the challenges facing Britain and Europe. Current programmes cover the areas of economic and industrial policy, Europe, governmental reform, human rights, defence, social policy, the environment and media issues.

Besides its programme of research and publication, IPPR also provides a forum for political and trade union leaders, academic experts and those from business, finance, government and the media, to meet and discuss issues of common concern.

Trustees

Lord Eatwell (Chairman)
Gail Rebuck (Secretary)
Lord Gavron (Treasurer)
Lord Alli
Professor Tony Atkinson
Professor Kumar Bhattacharyya
Rodney Bickerstaffe
Lord Brooke

James Cornford
John Edmonds
Professor Anthony Giddens
Jeremy Hardie
Lord Hollick
Sir Jeremy Isaacs
Professor David Marquand
Jan Royall

Production & design by **EMPHASIS**
ISBN 1 86030 095 2
© IPPR 1999
Printed and bound in Great Britain by Biddles Ltd, www.Biddles.co.uk

Contents

Preface

IPPR's report *The Entrepreneurial Society* was launched by Tony Blair in May 1998. It was well received and contributed to a whole host of policy areas ranging from the role of enterprise in the education system to the provision of advice and support for new companies.

As Labour's first term progresses, the role of small firms has risen even higher up the agenda with policies aimed at encouraging entrepreneurship and at changing incentives for small company investment. Most recently the Government has embarked on a consultation to establish a Small Business Service, an attempt to put the concerns of small businesses more firmly at the heart of government.

This report is in many respects our response to that consultation process. It was originally designed as a follow-up to *The Entrepreneurial Society*, aiming to look at the role of government support towards growing small companies and at the ways in which more firms could be encouraged to realise their potential. In order to inform the policy recommendations we carried out two pieces of research, one investigating the growth programmes offered by Business Links and another addressing how sectoral differences impact on the design and delivery of support services for small companies. We have not looked specifically at 'macro' policies such as finance or taxation except where these impact on different types of company or sector.

We have also drawn out the implications for the future development of support services in order to stimulate further discussion and on-going debate. The work has already contributed to discussions within the Department of Culture, Media and Sport and input into a working group set up to investigate the specific issues facing small companies in the music industry.

Acknowledgements

We would like to give our grateful thanks to our two sponsors, the DTI SME Policy Unit and Kingston Smith Chartered Accountants.

Several people were also extremely helpful during the course of the project, particularly Michael Snyder, Kingston Smith Chartered Accountants; Maria Kenyon, DTI; Claire Martin, NatWest; Geraint Howells, Ben Howe, Ed Bayley, all of Kingston Smith Chartered Accountants; Alison Wenham, AIM; Sarah Taylor, Institute of Management Consultancy; Mike Hopkins, BPIF; John Connaughton, Davis Langdon Consultancy; Helen Morrell, Business Link Directorate, DTI. Many other people contributed to seminars at the IPPR and gave their time for interviews.

About the authors

Andrea Westall is Research Fellow at the IPPR. She was part of the secretariat for the Commission on Public Policy and British Business which produced its final report *Promoting Prosperity* in 1997. She co-authored a major study of new businesses, *The Entrepreneurial Society*, and has been involved in a variety of government initiatives designed to promote entrepreneurship. Her other research interests include regeneration, corporate responsibility, and social exclusion. Future work at IPPR will focus on self-employment; the role of mutuals, co-operatives and not-for-profits in public-private partnerships; and the relationship between microenterprises and regeneration strategies.

Marc Cowling recently became Director of the Research Centre for Industrial Strategy at Birmingham University Business School where he heads a team looking at issues relating to SME development, competitiveness and public policy. In the last 12 months he has been an expert advisor to the Treasury review of SME financing, the DTI Small Firms Loan Guarantee Scheme evaluation and the OECD SME best practice working party. He is currently evaluating the economic impact of unemployment to self-employment initiatives for the DfEE.

Summary of recommendations

While smaller companies are crucial parts of dynamic markets and create opportunities for enterprising people, there are still barriers to their growth and sustainability which mean that they may not be achieving their potential. This underperformance therefore results in small firms contributing less to job creation and growth within the UK economy than could be the case. These barriers to growth are variously described as coming from sources external to the firm, as a result of being small *per se*, or as linked to the aspirations and capabilities of the owner-managers themselves.

Much current policy is directed towards reducing these barriers, for example, at reducing problems of access to finance or increasing innovation. But there is a tendency for policy to adopt a manufacturing model of business rather than to recognise the diversity of small businesses. Policy solutions tend to adopt a 'one size fits all' approach and do not take into account the impact of differences between small firms. Such heterogeneity relates to sector, size, age or business models, which include virtual networks of the self-employed or temporary project-based links between companies. Business support and small firm policy could have far more impact if it understands and adapts to this diversity.

There is also a tendency to divide firms into growth and 'lifestyle' businesses. Lifestyle businesses are defined as being those that do not seek growth but where the owner-manager just seeks to obtain a comfortable income. But our research shows that having a motivation towards lifestyle does not necessarily have any impact on the ability or desire to grow or create jobs. However, it is true that many self-employed and micro-enterprises do not wish to grow. Our work indicates that more could be done to encourage a greater proportion of such companies to embark on a growth trajectory. Motivations, particularly towards growth, matter. We give examples of initiatives which are explicitly aimed at changing culture and realising growth.

But we cannot see growth as just being internalised to individual firms. Growth arises from sets of inter-relationships between companies both within and across sectors. Much greater attention needs to be paid to encouraging more networking between public and private sector players at local, regional and national level both to spread knowledge and encourage more self-help responses. This approach is made even more imperative with the increased speed of innovation and dynamism of markets – static and reactive business support cannot hope to have all the answers.

The way to encourage more businesses to access advice and support is to provide a whole range of access points which work for different types of companies both to increase the engagement of the small business sector but also to create customised services. This means that the future Small Business Service will have to work in partnership with finance providers, accountants, solicitors, further and higher education, the RDAs and other public and private sector business support and training providers.

Motivations and growth

It is critical to address motivations and explore how business success as defined by owner-managers relates to desirable outcomes for policy-makers and the economy. When small business owners are asked about the barriers to growth, they tend to refer to problems outside the firm such as increasing market competition, but many of these perceived external barriers often relate to their own individual capabilities and skills. And they also relate to their motivations.

We found that having a growth orientation substantially increases the likelihood of achieving growth but that having a profit orientation does not necessarily result in increased profit. But while 60 per cent of those surveyed had some growth orientation, a smaller proportion actually achieved growth, therefore indicating other external and internal barriers. We also found that businesspeople hold a variety of motivations for running their business at the same time – such as the desire for independence and lifestyle alongside desiring to grow or becoming more profitable. Our research shows that if you ask owner-managers whether they have a lifestyle orientation, for example, there is no necessary impact on subsequent growth and profitability.

We also found that:

●   Micro firms are the least likely to wish to grow or introduce product innovations.

●   Product innovators are more motivated by profits and growth than non-innovators.

- Firms controlled by the founding entrepreneur are less likely to innovate.

- Firms that network are more likely to innovate.

- Growing firms generate higher profits than non-growers.

A review of the growth orientations of Business Link users prior to and after they received support, gave some strong results. Rapid growth companies were remarkably similar in their characteristics to companies who wanted to stay the same, indicating that growth is a deliberate choice. The business support provided also appeared to, on average, increase future growth orientation. This effect was most pronounced for those who had previously wanted to downsize – 62 per cent of whom now wanted to grow.

We also found several examples of innovative schemes, provided mostly by enterprise agencies, which indicate that it is possible to change growth orientations. Techniques include encouraging owner-managers to recognise skill and business deficiencies by using customers to identify problems or using peer groups of micro-enterprises to enable firms to set goals and targets for future performance and to implement strategies to accomplish these.

Evaluation of Business Link support

We conducted a survey of Business Link support and its effectiveness. The findings indicate that most services provided are attracting firms at the upper end of the small firm range. There is therefore a gap (whether from marketing or take-up) in reaching the smallest firms, arguably those in most need of support. The evidence also suggests that on average, business support and advice provided by Business Links has been successful in helping SMEs to grow, making firms more profitable and increasing sales while having a smaller but still significant impact on job creation.

Evaluation

- Less than half of the BL service providers were able to provide any final impact measures. This is surprising given the importance of such information for the ongoing development of programmes.

The DTI Business Link Performance Assessment Unit has now introduced a requirement for business support agencies to provide impact figures and therefore this situation should be changing.

- Evaluation of SME initiatives seems to be more *ad hoc*, less systematic, and much more variable in quality than in many other countries. Techniques used by BLs range from so called 'happy face/sad face' methods to more sophisticated survey methods and statistical analysis. We realise that the business imperatives on BLs mean that they find it hard to find the time or money to undertake such work but it is important to have comparable rigorous data across BLs to enable future planning of appropriate support services. There is also great variation in the technical rigour applied to national evaluations, which range from the presentation of basic data to advanced econometric methods. Often this reflects the relative abilities of particular types of contractors to undertake detailed statistical analysis.

- Funds for evaluation are low when compared to the annual costs of many schemes and the potential benefits derived from proper evaluation. One recent, and large scale, evaluation in the UK had a budget which approximated to only 0.17 per cent of the annual costs of the scheme.

- Business Links have recently been equipped with Client Management Systems (CMSs) which are databases that track client details over time including the type of intervention they received and any changes in their performance. However, it is not clear that the BLs are using these systems effectively since many could not provide us with the data required to permit full evaluation of schemes. The proper use of the CMSs should substantially reduce the cost of evaluation and permit more real-time, longitudinal impact studies.

Identifying and targeting firms

- The methods which BLs use to target firms are varied and to a large extent *ad hoc*.

- Less than 25 per cent of BLs use databases to identify, for example, growth firms. This suggests that they are not making full use of existing, national on-line company databases.

The reliance on the Personal Business Advisor in finding appropriate clients for support, suggests that currently there is no clear approach to identifying firms which is based on good market data. The lack of localised, or national, registers of businesses means that resources are wasted in trying to identify firms which would be likely to benefit from the provision of support.

It is likely that a more innovative and proactive approach to attracting new customers to BLs will encourage those firms who are the least likely to seek out advice and support and where the greatest impacts could be made. Methods of encouraging more firms to make use of services could involve increased links between BLs and banks and accountants in order to encourage referrals and the use of business clubs and networks as ways of drawing more people into a culture of accessing external advice and support.

Bias

Recent studies have shown that the take-up of services is significantly biased towards manufacturing. While there are a whole host of reasons why this might be the case, this discrepancy exists and confirms the point made above that support is too heavily focused on manufacturing and influenced by its models of growth and business practice.

Taking a sectoral approach

In order to investigate this manufacturing bias we held a series of seminars on different sectors – printing, music, and management consultancy. It was clear that although there are generic barriers to growth, there are often specific issues relevant to a sector and even to particular subsectors. At the very least, this complexity requires that there are appropriate statistics and adequate knowledge of the issues facing small firms within sectors and subsectors.

However, obvious difficulties with this approach arise straight away – sectors hide a multitude of subsectors, and sector boundaries are constantly shifting and changing. In relation to policy support, a great deal of attention is currently being paid to clusters – groups of interrelated firms who may come from a variety of industries. But it is worth also paying attention to the particular sector because a key thread running through each of the seminars was that differences in industries matter because growing firms are embedded within different types of markets. Growth and growth strategies can mean different things in different industries as can the way in which barriers to growth such as access to finance or advice and support are manifested.

Take up of advice and support

It appears, and this was upheld by the experience of the sector studies, that many small business owners might be more receptive to advice being offered by people who know their industry. Although they acknowledge the importance and relevance of generic skills, it was felt that they might be more inclined to access training and support if it was more targeted.

Existing sectoral support such as specific development agencies or local network initiatives enable clients and members to respond very quickly to changing markets and they provide people with the information and contacts to find business opportunities. They can enable businesspeople to join together to find joint solutions and strategies as they arise, whether that is to accessing markets or creating appropriate learning opportunities. It therefore appears important to focus on the sector itself and create networks to encourage companies to build their capacity and respond to changes in market circumstances. In other words, the aim is to increase the capacity for self-help based on access to up-to-date knowledge of both markets and relevant support provision. Policy can help by encouraging such networks at national, regional or local level.

The design of policies

It is not clear to what extent policies which affect small firms are also tested for their impacts on different sectors. The IR35 proposal is a recent example of a policy which was driven by one set of industry conditions or model of business but which would inadvertently impact negatively on more legitimate ways of working. The idea behind IR35 is to reduce tax avoidance by preventing people from opting out of employed status (or being forced out of employment). However, a wide range of activities would be affected – for example, a photographic agency acting on behalf of photographers, management consultancy networks, IT and portfolio executive professionals and their intermediary companies.

The implementation of policies

There is a tendency to develop broad solutions to small firm issues, for example, the Small Firms Loan Guarantee Scheme and the proposed regional 'equity gap' funds. But there are many reasons why some small firms cannot or do not access loan finance or equity, including issues relevant to different types of industry.

Knowledge of sectors and the particular issues that arise can result in more appropriate implementation of proposals. In the area of equity, the US recognises the importance of taking a sectoral approach through more industry specific finance instruments and expert advisors. The analysis of the music industry particularly indicates a need to understand specific finance issues, for example, the attitude of finance providers to the sector or reasons why firms do not use certain types of finance. It points to the potential to address these issues at the sectoral level through, for example, sector business angels and mentors. Other approaches include the consideration of industry-specific financial instruments and creating opportunities for dialogue between finance providers and the industry to increase understanding and develop solutions to specific problems.

Implications for the future of the Small Business Service and business support

The Small Business Service needs to greatly increase its understanding of the diversity of small businesses and use this information when advising on the development of existing and future legislation which affects small business. It is no good just to 'think small' it also necessary to consider the trade-offs and balances of legislation for different industries and different sizes and forms of firms. There needs to be a great deal of research into such diversity in order not to repeat some of the mistakes of previous generic small firm policies.

The DTI has said that the Small Business Service will listen more to small firms. In order to reflect the diversity of small firms and access the views of the self-employed and micro-enterprises who are under-represented by existing lobby groups or trade associations, it will be necessary to ensure that all groups are represented and consulted. This may mean creating new interest groups and accessing underrepresented small firms through surveys and focus groups at the national, regional and local level.

There is a need to engage more businesspeople in seeking external advice and support. It is not at all clear that the proposed model for the Small Business Service will be adequate or appropriate to significantly increase the numbers accessing advice. There should be more attention to using innovative approaches to drawing in more businesses through, for example, peer group networks, or perhaps roadshows (building on the Scottish Enterprise Personal Enterprise Shows). New technology can of course be used to provide access points to information and to on-line advice and helplines. We have already seen that sectors and clusters are other ways to engage people.

Both the Small Business Service and the Regional Development Agencies (RDAs) will need the capability and capacity to create networks between support providers (whether public and private). It is not clear yet that they have the appropriate remit or flexible resources to engage in enough of such activity even though the RDAs have set out some clear and workable strategies within their development plans.

Although there has been increased local flexibility in business support, the proposed franchise approach to delivering the Small Business Service may break up existing critical partnerships which are necessary to identify appropriate needs and solutions. There is probably therefore a need to build on, or create where necessary, stable sub-regional strategic partnerships that involve all key players such as finance providers, local authorities, business representatives, and voluntary sector bodies which can cross-cut the business support, training and regeneration agendas.

It is very clear that future business support is going to have to be highly flexible and responsive to rapidly changing markets. For that reason it is appropriate to embed more of it within peer group networks and within the realities of markets. The use of new technologies will enable this process but, as our seminars demonstrated, the key is to increase understanding of different small firm needs and increase dialogue between all relevant groups so that solutions can be found. Government support bodies need the flexibility to be able to play a catalytic role and help create innovative and appropriate solutions to barriers to small firm growth.

Introduction

The Government's attention to small firms in the economy has increased as evidence has accumulated of their contributions to job creation, innovation, and the growth and dynamism of industries and of regions. But at the same time, there has been concern that not enough small companies seek growth, and particularly high growth.

This argument is justified by using broad comparative statistics across countries, such as the high number of self-employed without employees in the UK compared to elsewhere. But these comparisons can tell us very little because there are such huge differences between economies. A more fruitful line of enquiry is to look at barriers to growth, to find out why small firms are not achieving their potential and to understand the complexity of small firms and the variety of business models.

The fact that there are barriers to growth indicates that there is the possibility of more job creation and GDP growth from small firms. It is also useful to question the attitudes to growth of owner-managers, and to ask whether more of those who currently do not want to grow, might do so given some encouragement. This report focuses particularly on how government might encourage more firms to grow and how it might persuade and enable more firms to access appropriate and timely advice and support.

We also take a broad view of the relationship of small firms to growth and job creation. Whilst it is true that high growth small and medium-sized companies (SMEs) contribute disproportionately to job creation, self-employment, micro-enterprises, small, medium and large firms, and their interrelationships, are all important to the growth and vitality of industries[1]. Government has tended to focus most of its business support on high growth firms but small firm growth can mean different things in different sectors. Growth may sometimes be better seen in the context of networks of activity rather than just arising from individual firms. In management consultancy, for example, there are a whole range of possible business models including networks of self-employed professionals who may join together for particular projects or a core small firm linked with many associates.

Another aspect of our work is to explore the diversity of small businesses, understand these differences and incorporate that knowledge into policy making. However, much academic analysis, and therefore policy responses informed by that work, have focused predominantly on traditional manufacturing where industries tend to be characterised by the dominance and higher productivity of large companies. Hence policy has been biased towards a certain view of small firms and the issues concerning their growth, resulting in policies that may not be relevant to many companies.

The policy context

The Government has responded in a variety of ways to tackle these barriers to growth for small firms. For example, the proposed Small Business Service has been set up to:

● Act as a voice for small business at the heart of Government.

● Simplify and improve the quality and coherence of Government support for small businesses.

● Help small firms deal with regulation and ensure small firms' interests are properly considered in future regulation (DTI, 1999a).

There is a whole raft of policy proposals, many of which were initiated by the previous government, aimed at tackling problems of access to finance, for example, the Small Firms Loan Guarantee Scheme (to provide bank loans for companies without collateral or a track record), and the Enterprise Investment Scheme (to encourage equity investment in new and small companies). RDAs also have been charged with creating a coherent business support infrastructure in their regions alongside encouraging businesses to increase the skill levels of their workforces.

The Regional Development Agencies are currently being invited to submit proposals for regional equity funds in order to fill the equity gap – the gap between the demand and supply for venture capital particularly for high-growth and innovative small firms. IPPR is exploring the rationale for this particular policy and its potential impact in another report (Harding, 1999).

Attention has also been focused on encouraging entrepreneurship and the creation of new businesses. For example, the DTI's 1998 Competitiveness White Paper announced a National Campaign for

Enterprise to promote entrepreneurship (including within schools and universities); and promised enhanced business support through Business Links for at least 10,000 start-ups by 2001.

There has also been increasing attention to the role of businesses in regeneration and tackling social exclusion. The New Deal now incorporates support for self-employment and the Social Exclusion Unit has been focusing on the role of small businesses in regeneration and the need for microcredit facilities to support their growth. A recent area of interest has been in encouraging older people to set up businesses both to decrease the inactivity rates (particularly amongst older men) and to harness the expertise of some mature people who could contribute to the growth of new and existing companies.

What we aimed to do

In order to inform current policy debates, particularly with respect to the Small Business Service, we sought to address the following questions:

- *Could more people be encouraged to grow their companies?* (Chapter 2)

    We used a survey of firms conducted in 1995 and analysed the results to investigate the impact of owner-manager motivations on the subsequent growth of the company. Our research shows that lifestyle motivations do not necessarily preclude growth, and that, therefore, it may well be possible to encourage some businesses which are currently low- or no-growth to increase their activity. We also looked at the impact on the growth orientations of owner-managers before and after taking up Business Link support and explored a variety of innovative schemes aimed at encouraging more people to seek more growth and job creation.

- *How effective is current business support and could more businesspeople be encouraged to take up advice and training?* (Chapter 3)

    We undertook a survey of Business Link support and its effects on the subsequent growth of firms. We also set out a variety of ways in which government's role may have to change in order to encourage firms to seek out advice and support.

●   *Are generic small firm policies adequate to deal with the diversity of small firms?* (Chapter 4 and case studies)

We explored the implications of taking on a more complex view of small firms for policy by holding a series of seminars to explore barriers to growth in different industries. We particularly focused on issues such as access to finance and the take-up of advice and support.

Chapter 1 sets the scene by looking at the relationship between small firms and the economy and the particular barriers which may hold back smaller companies from achieving their potential.

1 Small firms and growth

Introduction

Whilst there is wide recognition of the importance of small firms to the economy, there has been a tendency in academic and policy circles to focus on high growth or 'potential high growth' companies, those believed to create most of the jobs and contribute most to growth. But growth depends on a range of factors including innovation, creating niche markets, and collaboration between companies.

We also have to be very careful about what we mean when we talk about the growth of small firms. Growth can be measured in a number of ways. Indicators used include job creation, turnover, and profitability. But these measurements do not necessarily all point in the same direction. Growth measured by profitability, for example, may not necessarily run alongside either increase in turnover or employment. In order to achieve higher profits in the future, some firms can just become more efficient by using their existing resources more productively.

This chapter sets out the ways in which small firms contribute to growth and job creation. It also addresses the question of whether there could be more growth from the small firm sector and analyses some of the evidence that is put forward to justify this position. It then goes on to look at the factors that are associated with growth and some of the most common barriers faced by small firm owner-managers.

How do small firms contribute to growth and job creation?

There is a wealth of literature that illustrates the complex role of small firms within the economy. The OECD (1996) workshop on SMEs: Employment, Innovation and Growth summarised these findings and pointed to the distinct role of new and small firms in economic growth. For example:

> Major structural shifts often involve the development of new economic sectors and are frequently indicated by the appearance of large numbers of small firms... Under some conditions and for certain types of economic production, a

vigorous new and small firm sector is not an aberration, but a necessity for a competitive regional economy... There are numerous examples of individual regions or industrial districts, dominated by SMEs, that appear to have led to substantial economic growth for these districts... Small firms are either a mechanism for transmitting economic growth or an independent source of growth – a source of economic growth not provided by larger firms... The presence of smaller firms is associated with economic sector growth, even when the overall sector, manufacturing, may be in decline.

They also noted that:

- New and small firms provide a disproportionate share of gross and net new jobs.

- Firm and job turbulence are a necessary feature of economic growth.

- New and small firms appear to play an important role in the development of innovation.

This work indicates that it is not just small firms who grow to large or medium-sized that contribute to economic growth and job creation but that small firms in their own right play important parts in dynamic economies. This point is often missed in small firm policy, which tends to focus mainly on high growth firms. Both the growth of individual firms and the growth and job creation arising from the interrelationships between the self-employed, micro, small, medium and large firms are equally important. Too often the focus has been on the individual firm in isolation rather than seeing it as embedded in sets of business relationships.

What is the evidence for a shortfall in growth and job creation amongst small firms?

A comment often made is that the UK has more self-employed without employees than many other countries. In Great Britain, only 29 per cent of the self-employed are 'job creators'. Table 1.1 outlines the respective proportions of job creators across a broad spectrum of

European countries. It is striking that Great Britain has the third lowest proportion of self-employed job-creators. Only Spain and Greece do worse. Countries such as Germany, Luxembourg, Austria and Denmark all have very much higher job creation rates.

Table 1.1 Self-employed with employees for different European countries

	percentage of total self-employed with employees[1]	percentage labour force who are self-employed[2]
West Germany	52	n/a
Luxembourg	52	9.1
Austria	47	10.8
Denmark	45	8.3
Ireland	41	19.8
Holland	39	11.2
Italy	39	24.8
Belgium	37.5	15.4
Portugal	34	26.8
France	31	11.3
Great Britain	29	12.6
Spain	28.5	21.5
Greece	27	33.7

1: Source: European Foundation for the Improvement of Living and Working Conditions, Survey, 1996.

2: Source: Employment in Europe, 1999, EC Employment and Social Affairs (data for 1996)

But do we really know why these discrepancies exist across countries? The self-employed are not a homogenous group: only a small proportion will conform to the model of the classic businessperson who might be able to take on employees. Types of self-employment range from knowledge professionals to the 'pseudo-self-employed' – people who are virtually indistinguishable from employees. Only by understanding such breakdowns across countries and sectors could we hope to make any meaningful comparisons. And there are wide differences between the proportions of self-employment in different countries as a percentage of the workforce. The countries at the top of the list in Table 1.1 have, on balance relatively lower numbers of the self-employed and so the actual numbers of job-creating self-employed may well be lower or similar to countries further down the list. However, there is no direct relation between high number of job-creating self-employed people and low overall self-employment. Ireland for example has 19.8 per cent of the workforce in self-employment but 41 per cent of these are job creators.

But perhaps we should not be too worried about the proportion of the job-creating self-employed. Evidence indicates the importance of self-employment in its own right. A recent Swedish study showed that, when the numbers of the self-employed increase by one per cent of the workforce, total employment increases by 0.5 per cent in the short-run and by 1.3 per cent in the long run. The implication here is that the self-employed do not just replace existing waged employment (Folster, 1999).

But there are barriers for the self-employed who might want to take on employees. It is well known that the hardest thing to do is to take on the first employee, but that once that decision is made, it is very rarely reversed (Carroll *et al*, 1996). Recently, a successful project in Wales, TARGED, the Sole Traders Initiative, run by two TECs, enabled small businesses to acquire guidance and help with the business needs and administration involved in taking on that first employee. The Employment Service matched the firm's needs with the skills and competencies available in the local labour market.

We also know that about two thirds of the self-employed do not wish to grow and only want to achieve a certain level of income for themselves (Taylor, 1996). Many of these people are deemed to run 'lifestyle' businesses that do not grow. But, as we shall see in Chapter Three, it is not possible to always equate a lifestyle orientation with no growth since there is evidence that lifestyle motivations do not preclude actual or desired growth in many small firms and micro-enterprises. This fact might suggest that more effort could be made to encourage more of the self-employed who could grow to do so.

Another widely accepted and related area of concern is the small size of our 'Mittelstand' or number of medium-sized companies compared to elsewhere. However, if you look at Figure 1.1, there is little difference between say France, Germany and the UK in the amount of employment accounted for by firms with 50-249 employees. Government has tended to pick on statistics that refer solely to manufacturing when expressing concern about the Mittelstand. It is not clear whether these differences are explained by different business models, for example, increased outsourcing, rather than to any relatively different abilities of smaller firms to grow.

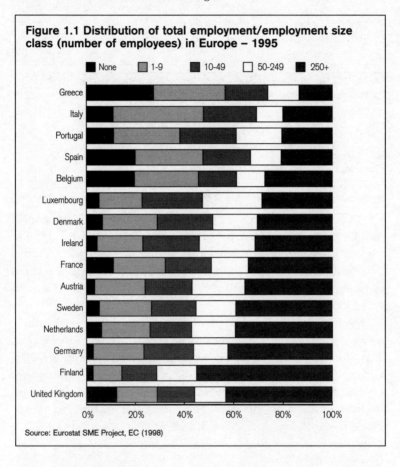

Figure 1.1 Distribution of total employment/employment size class (number of employees) in Europe – 1995

Source: Eurostat SME Project, EC (1998)

The implication behind the concern over the Mittelstand is that not enough firms survive and grow to become medium or large size companies. This presumes that the larger the company the greater the market power, export potential and productivity. However, although it is true that, in general, productivity does rise with the size of company, there is no easy relationship between size and efficiency across sectors. Data on two broad groups of UK businesses illustrate this point. Table 1.2 on manufacturing shows that, the larger the company, the more its

---

Table 1.2 Breakdown of manufacturing firms by size of company

| | Size (number of employees) | | | | |
	None	*1-49*	*50-249*	*250+*	*Total*
Employment (%)	5.1	23.8	20.7	50.5	100.1
Turnover (%)	1.4	18.1	17.3	63.2	100

Source: DTI, 1999b

Table 1.3 Breakdown of real estate, business activities (broad grouping of service industry sectors) by size of company

| | Size (number of employees) | | | | |
	None	*1-49*	*50-249*	*250+*	*Total*
Employment (%)	15.4	42.3	12.9	29.4	100
Turnover (%)	6.5	51.1	14.9	27.4	99.9

Source: DTI, 1999b

---

impact on turnover relative to its impact on employment. For example, manufacturing firms account for 63.2 per cent of turnover but only 50.5 per cent of employment. For more service-oriented companies, (Table 1.3), firms in the 1-49 size category have a disproportionate impact on turnover than on employment. But it must be said that these are very broad statistics.

Finer breakdowns of sectors illustrate a variety of relationships between turnover and employment share and size of company. There is also a body of evidence that suggests that small firms can generate above normal profits by targeting niche markets where the advantages of being large are not so noticeable (Bradburd and Ross, 1990), again illustrating the trade-offs between growth and profitability. Such relationships are not new. Penrose, back in 1959, assumed that small firms iterate towards some sort of equilibrium size where they are at their most efficient.

However, as we shall see below, there are substantive barriers to growth for small companies, which also suggests that there is some potential for more growth and job creation. The self-employed and micro-enterprises show the least tendency to wish to grow. We know that, of those companies that do not grow when young, many will die or stay very small. Two thirds of firms who are at least ten years old are still micro-enterprises[2]. However, it must be remembered that, despite their lack of growth, such firms contribute to sustainable job creation.

Table 1.4 Percentage of growing or stable/declining firms (measured by employment)

	Size (number of employees)			
	Micro <10	Small 10-49	Medium 50-249	Large 250+
Stable/declining	74.5	42.1	43.2	32.3
Growing	25.5	57.9	56.8	67.7

Source: Westhead and Cowling, Warwick Business School, 1995

Table 1.5 Percentage of growing or stable/declining firms (measured by sales)

	Size (number of employees)			
	Micro	Small	Medium	Large
Stable/declining	33.3	28.7	29.4	27.3
Growing	66.7	71.3	70.6	72.7

Source: Westhead and Cowling, Warwick Business School, 1995

The breakdown, shown in Table 1.4, indicates the numbers of companies who were stable/declining or growing as measured by employment growth. It illustrates the point made above that the majority of micro firms do not wish to, and do not, grow.

However, the picture changes somewhat when you look at real sales growth. Table 1.5 shows that two-thirds of micro firms are growing in sales revenue (at least to some extent). That fact illustrates the continued viability of such businesses even if they do not increase their employment.

Another point of concern, as shown in *The Entrepreneurial Society* (Gavron *et al*, 1998), is that the UK has one of the worst survival rates of new small firms in the OECD (Table 1.6) – 30 per cent survival after five years in 1994 compared with 42 per cent for France and 58 per cent for Ireland. However, most firms that close do so voluntarily rather than through bankruptcy. We do not know if that percentage varies across countries. There are a variety of positive reasons for exit, the most obvious of which is selling on a successful company. Cressy and Storey (1995) point out that 52 per cent of a cohort of 2000 start-ups ceased trading but under one third of those closed because of insolvency. Comparable evidence from the British Household Panel

Table 1.6 Length of survival of newly-created enterprises (in percentages) 1988-94

Country	Birth	1 year	2 years	3 years	4 years	5 years	6 years
Denmark	100				69	58	
France	100	83	69	58	50	42	
Germany	100	90	81	73	68	62	
Ireland	100	90	80	70	63	58	
Sweden	100			66			
UK	100	80	61	48	36	30	
US	100		76		48		38
US *1-4emp*	100						37
US *>4emp*	100						49

Notes: The high survival rate for Germany probably reflects the fact that new entrepreneurs have to pass an examination before they can set up a business.

Source: OECD Employment Outlook, 1994.

Survey (Taylor, 1997) shows that only 17.2 per cent of those exiting from self-employment did so involuntarily.

So, although we have to be careful about what we mean by the lack of growth of small firms, it does appear that there could be more job creation and growth than is currently the case. We know that there are difficulties with being small. A host of studies indicate that many firms fail or underperform because they are either undercapitalised or have poor management capacity (Gavron *et al*, 1998). The reasons range from the inability to access finance on appropriate terms, to lack of training of staff and poor financial and business skills of the owner-managers. Smaller companies also tend to be less technologically sophisticated and undertake less research and development (R&D) and innovation. Much small firm policy has been directed at attempting to address these deficits through, for example, regional innovation strategies, R&D tax credits, Business Links, the Small Firm Loan Guarantee Scheme or the Enterprise Investment Scheme.

Growth matters

Economic theory tends to predict that newer and smaller firms need to grow in order to survive and the evidence supports this position. There

Table 1.7 Growth and start-up survival rates

No of employees at start-up	*Percentage of start-ups surviving to year 6*				
	Zero growth	Low growth	Medium growth	High growth	All
1 to 4	26.0	65.0	75.6	77.2	37.2
5 to 499	34.1	72.4	75.3	79.2	49.2
All firms	27.5%	66.3%	75.5%	78.4%	39.8%

is a positive correlation between growth and survival (Reynolds, 1993). Phillips and Kirchoff (1989) illustrate a strong and direct relationship between even low growth and survival. Table 1.7 indicates the findings.

The contribution of high growth

High growth small firms have been the focus of policy because they are believed to create the greatest number of new jobs. This was particularly important recently since employment in large companies has been contracting. However, more recent statistics indicate that both small and large companies create jobs but there are huge sectoral differences (Table 1.8). The DTI, in comments to IPPR on this data, noted that:

> between 1993 and 1997 employment in the 500+ employee size band declined in most sectors in line with the trend since the early 1980s of greater concentration of jobs in SMEs. Two exceptions are Wholesale & Retail and Hotels & Catering which have both seen increased market concentration in recent years.

Table 1.8 Employment change, 1993-1997, by size of business

Size (no of employees)	Employment end-1993	Employment start-1997	Change 1993-97
0	3,017,000	2,866,000	-151,000
1-49	6,069,000	6,551,000	+482,000
50-249	2,862,000	2,544,000	-318,000
250+	8,661,000	9,112,000	+451,000
All	**20,607,000**	**21,073,000**	**+466,000**

Source: DTI

It is true that on average only a certain small percentage of firms will account for most job creation. For example, Storey's seminal work showed that over a ten-year period only four per cent of new firms contributed 50 per cent of jobs created (Storey, 1994)[3]. Gallagher and Miller (1991) identified firms called 'flyers' – 18 per cent of firms who contributed 92 per cent of job creation over about six years in the South East.

But, as pointed out in *The Entrepreneurial Society* (Gavron *et al*, 1998), there are several problems with presuming that the implication of the above analysis is just to support potential (or actual) growth companies:

●   It is just as difficult to predict which firms will or will not be growth firms as it is to predict successful or growth start-ups.

●   Even if only four per cent of SMEs currently generate most of the new jobs, any increase in the supply of new businesses enlarges the pool from which growth firms will emerge.

●   Four per cent is not necessarily fixed. There might be barriers or hurdles which result in a low percentage of firms surviving or growing or which act to discourage people who could create viable new businesses. Removing or easing these would push up the ratio.

Also, it can quite clearly be shown that new firms also contribute to GDP growth in other ways through, for example, innovation, increased competition and contributing to the growth of new industries (see Gavron et al, 1998). The results of that analysis lent support to recent policy attention towards promoting a more entrepreneurial culture, devising business birth-rate strategies in some RDA regional economic strategies and addressing barriers to starting up in business including access to bank finance and equity. More recently, the Social Exclusion Unit has also been focussing on the role of micro-enterprises and new businesses within regeneration strategies.

One of the strongest indications of the role of new enterprises in regional development comes from recent evidence from the UK and the US (Reynolds *et al*, 1994; Gallagher and Botham, 1998) that regions with high business birthrates, all other things considered, tend to have higher rates of GDP growth and job creation. However, there are no studies investigating whether regions, sectors or countries with more high growth companies (as defined by job creation) also have higher GDP growth. As noted earlier, growth arises from a variety of factors.

This point is part of a broader concern. Much work on high growth companies tends only to focus on growth as defined by job creation. There is very little analysis of how small firms and growing firms impact on growth in terms of GDP whether in sectors, in regions or in countries.

Another difficulty with studies of high-growth companies is that, although the results are quite compelling, they probably underestimate the number of potential growth companies. Recent work by the OECD (1998a) has shown that the trajectory of the average high growth firm follows a gradual incremental increase in its workforce over time. However, this picture is only an average of the activity of many firms. It hides the fact that, for most companies, expansion is not continuous and firms can experience increases as well as falls in the size of their workforce. An implication is that growth, over the last three years, for example, is not necessarily an indicator of future growth and neither does lack of growth in the previous three years condemn the firm to no further growth, or even high growth. Support providers have therefore to be extremely careful about the way in which they classify and identify 'potential growth' companies.

If growth is measured by non-employment criteria such as turnover, the same results occur. Smallbone *et al* (1995), for example, showed that high growth firms are spread across sectors and a firm's growth orientation may change over time due to specific triggers such as a leadership change or external events. Again, policies that depend on historical growth criteria or on specific characteristics of the company or owner-managers, would miss businesses that were capable of growing, given a change in one or more parameters.

High growth companies are found across all sectors (including those in decline) but are not uniformly distributed – the service sector shows a significantly higher proportion of high-growth firms than manufacturing. The OECD (1998b) recently looked at the contribution of high-growth firms defined as the product of absolute and relative changes in employment and found that altogether, high growth firms accounted for between two and ten per cent of permanent firms. In all countries, over three-quarters of high growth firms were SMEs

(HGSMEs). These HGSMEs accounted for the bulk of net job creation in most countries except for the Netherlands where most net job creation came from large firms. In France, Canada, Italy and Spain, between 53 and 66 per cent of high growth firms are concentrated in five industries.

Is supporting high-tech the solution?

In the UK, work has pointed to the strength of new technology based firms (NTBFs) which appear to have a much higher survival rate and are more likely to export (CBI, 1997). However, it must be noted that high tech is still only a small (albeit growing) percentage of the economy. The OECD (1997) report suggests that only about ten per cent of SMEs are technology based. Oakey (1995) noted that there are substantial sectoral differences amongst NTBFs and that:

> a universal policy towards high technology small firms will probably not work. Whilst it may be appropriate to one specific sector, it may be damaging to other sectors. In extreme circumstances, a general solution may not benefit any sector.

For example, in the software sector, the emphasis for success may not be on technology but on strong marketing and management. The importance of taking sectoral differences into account are dealt with in Chapter Four.

This type of analysis indicates that it is important not to underestimate the importance of SMEs across the economy and to look at sectoral differences in barriers to growth.

Old or new firms?

There is a remarkable degree of consistency in the literature concerning the ability of newly established firms to create jobs (Barkham *et al*, 1996). Younger firms grow more rapidly than old, either reflecting a need to grow quickly to achieve a minimum efficient size or because older firms have less motivation to grow. However, it is dangerous to ignore mature firms – the implications of Smallbone's (1995) studies were that the potential of existing SMEs cannot be underestimated, particularly since growth is a discontinuous process. As we have seen, a firm's recent performance may not be a good indicator of future growth potential.

But it is also important to recognise the impact of mature firms on sustainable job creation and growth within an area, even those that are low or no growth. North and Smallbone (1994) argue that:

- Older companies show a high propensity to stay within their original locality or region) however, that is less true of the inner city).

- The threat of ownership changes such as take-over is minimal.

- Younger firms may be more likely to grow and contribute to job growth but established firms do so too.

- Some mature firms sell a substantial proportion of their goods outside the local area and tend to increase their involvement in wider geographical markets over time.

These points are particularly relevant to regeneration strategies which therefore should not just concentrate on promoting the formation of new businesses.

Motivations matter

Table 1.9 shows that around two thirds of business owners (excluding the self-employed) have no further ambition for their business than to generate moderate growth. Around one in five businesses have a

Table 1.9 Growth aspirations by size of firm (percentages)				
	Micro	Small	Medium	Large
Stay same	13.2	10.4	9.8	6.3
Decline	2.7	1.7	2.2	1.7
Moderate growth	65.7	64.3	55.2	63.6
Fast growth	17.0	22.9	32.2	27.8
Total	98.6*	99.3	99.4	99.4

Source: Cambridge Small Business Research Centre (1992)

* These totals do not add up to 100% due to rounding errors.

strong growth objective. However, only one in ten businesses actually achieve substantial and/or continuous growth (CSBR, 1992). We show in Chapter Two that these motivations towards growth have very significant impacts on actual growth. These statistics also illustrate the importance of barriers to growth particularly for those who wish to grow.

A survey by Aston University Business School (1990) explored some of the implications of such barriers. It reported that a much smaller number of small firms than is often assumed are content with their present size, and have no plans for major investments. The reason why other surveys have overestimated the number of firms desiring no or limited growth is that they have paid too little attention to the effects of constraints upon growth intentions and to the cycle of growth consolidation in small firms (again ignoring the fact that growth is not continuous). In other words, people may be put off growth by the perception that they cannot achieve it.

These sorts of findings suggest that there are two potential avenues in which public policy might be successful:

● 　For the group who express a desire to grow but fail to realise their ambitions there is a need to identify exactly why this is the case. Thus the emphasis here is on barriers to growth whether internal or external.

● 　For the companies with no strong growth objective, there may be a case for trying to effect a culture change, particularly amongst those who have similar characteristics to fast growing firms. This 'don't want to but could grow' category is an important element of the stock of existing businesses in the UK.

So what factors are associated with growth?

There is no unified theory about the determinants of small firm growth and it is unlikely that there can be due to the diversity of small firms.

Storey (1994) breaks up the factors associated with growth into three areas – those dealing with the entrepreneur, the firm and the strategy. A summary follows.

The entrepreneur

The key drivers to achieve growth are motivation, education and management experience, size of founding team and the mix of management skills. We can therefore identify the attributes of successful entrepreneurs and areas where policy could potentially make a difference. One example would be in the building of teams with the required balance of functional skills.

The firm

We have already noted that younger firms tend to grow more than older firms. Additionally, industrial sector and geographical location appear to exert strong effects on growth. And limited liability status, rather than sole trader or partnership, is associated with faster growth.

The strategy

The recruitment of outside managers is associated with faster growth as is the ability to raise external equity finance (something to which many founding entrepreneurs are averse). Those firms whose owners and managers seek external advice and information are also more likely to grow. There has been a mixed set of evidence with regards to the impact of training on owner managers but, more recently, evidence from a recent pilot study within the Small Firms Loan Guarantee Scheme showed that training can have a significant impact on survival and growth (KPMG, 1999).

These three areas are all ones in which the business support infrastructure, whether public or private, has a role to play. It is likely that if more firms run by founder entrepreneurs could manage to open up their capital and move away from management teams drawn entirely from the close family or internal candidates, then faster growth would result.

Growth is also associated with the ability to bring new products and services to market as well as to identify market niches where firms are shielded from competition. Also the importance of innovation and technological sophistication to growth supports the strong policy efforts (for example through regional innovation strategies) to increase technology transfer and R&D amongst small firms.

Barriers to growth

One of the most rigorous studies of barriers to growth was undertaken by a 1992 survey of over 1,900 businesses by the Cambridge Small Business Research Centre. These barriers are specified by businesspeople themselves. In descending order, firms ranked the obstacles as follows:

- Cost and availability of finance for expansion.

- Cost and availability of overdraft facilities.

- Overall growth of market demand.

- Increasing competition.

- Marketing and sales skills.

- Management skills.

- Skilled labour.

- Acquisition of new technology.

Paul Burns from the University of the South Bank[4], noted recently that in any such survey, the same issues appear at the top of the list – notably increased competition (or lack of demand in a recession) or availability and cost of finance for expansion. He pointed out that it is very important to realise that these perceived barriers may not necessarily reflect actual ones and that in many cases such barriers really relate to the constraints of the owner-manager themselves.

From a break down of studies of reported constraints to growth, he made some other points:

- Manufacturing SMEs face greater constraints in most areas than do service companies (generally because it is harder to set up and grow).

- Larger SMEs face greater constraints than do micro firms.

- Innovating SMEs report higher levels of constraints than do non-innovators.

- Larger SMEs rate inadequate management skills – and to a lesser extent, marketing and sales skills – exceptionally high as a constraint.

- Newer and fast-growing SMEs rate financial constraints as serious.

- Fast growing SMEs rate management skills and skilled labour shortages more highly.

But all these examples relate generally to small firms as a whole. We decided to investigate barriers to growth as they are manifested in different sectors. The results are reported in Chapter Four.

Conclusions

Growing companies tend to survive longer and, once some growth has been achieved, it is likely that they will want to grow more. But growth is not continuous, and therefore it is hard to predict who will or will not grow in future. Growth orientations can change over time and external triggers can lead to increased growth. In many markets, size really does matter but in some industries, however, the most efficient size for a company may be relatively small or issues of market power may be less relevant as new technologies provide easier access to markets or the ability to create customised products and services.

High growth small firms are important to the economy but growth whether measured by GDP or job creation comes from a wide range of new and existing small firms and the inter-relationships between them. High growth SMEs are found across all sectors of the economy (including declining industries) but tend to be concentrated in certain sectors, particularly in service industries.

Evidence suggests that:

- About three quarters of micro-enterprises are no growth in terms of employment although two thirds are growing as measured by sales, indicating their continued viability.

- Roughly half of small and medium sized firms are growing.

- Two thirds of the self-employed do not and do not wish to grow.

The reasons for no- or low-growth can either relate to internal and external barriers to growth or to the motivations of the owner-managers towards growth.

We know that many small firms do not achieve their potential because they are not particularly innovative and have poor financial or management skills. External barriers can relate to lack of suitable business premises, lack of skilled labour or difficulties in obtaining finance. Much support infrastructure is aimed at reducing some of these internal barriers, for example, in increasing financial literacy, promoting the acquisition of management skills, diversifying products, or encouraging firms to access advice and support and learn from peer groups.

Before further exploring barriers to growth, particularly in relation to seeking out external advice and support, we explore the motivations of owner-managers towards growth and other considerations to see how they impact on actual growth and whether it is possible to encourage more companies to seek growth.

2. What motivates the small business?

'Understanding what motivates entrepreneurs to start and sustain their ventures has been a critical factor in understanding the complete entrepreneurial process.' (Kuratko, Hornsby and Naffziger, 1997)

Introduction

There is a tendency in policy circles to distinguish between lifestyle companies and growth companies – between those firms that operate to achieve a comfortable target income (generally implying no growth) and those that desire continuous growth and expansion. But entrepreneurs and business owners operate with a variety of motivations and goals in which there are no easy distinctions. To have a lifestyle motivation does not automatically mean that you will not also want to seek growth. Therefore we have to distinguish carefully between those companies who do not grow and are called 'lifestyle' and those business-owners who have lifestyle orientations to their business (not all of whom will be no growth). It is very important to address the question of what motivates business owners before looking at any other internal or external barriers to growth. As we noted in Chapter 1, the chief barrier to growth is often the owner-manager themselves and no growth programme can succeed in the long term if it does not attempt to alter the owner-managers' attitudes and capabilities.

Gray (1998) shows a direct relationship between profit as a motivation and firm size and an equally strong, but inverse, relationship between size and lifestyle objectives. In conclusion he states that: 'on the whole, we can sum up the small enterprise culture as one of aversion to growth, but favouring a strong sense of personal independence'.

It is therefore critical to address the motivations of owner-managers and explore how business success is defined by the owners of independent firms in order to attempt to reconcile this with the outcomes that are desirable for policy-makers and for the economy. Gray's comment supports the predominant view that it is better to support potential growth or already growing firms. But this approach does not address the question of whether it is possible to encourage and support more companies to seek sustained growth. We noted before that more firms desire growth than was previously thought and in this chapter we note that lifestyle orientations do not necessarily preclude growth. Policy therefore has to find innovative ways of working with owner-managers to unlock their potential.

This chapter has three sections. Firstly, we look at a study conducted by Marc Cowling and Paul Westhead which explores the motivations of owner-managers of small businesses, then we further explore a recent review of the impact of Business Link interventions and show the strong effects on the growth orientations of firms and finally we present some case studies of business support practice which seek to change the culture of companies and their attitudes towards growth.

The impact of motivations

In order to investigate how motivations interact with business success and growth, we have chosen to look at some results from a UK survey conducted amongst a representative sample of smaller, independent businesses (excluding the self-employed) which have been trading for a minimum of ten years. The survey, sponsored by the Leverhulme Trust, was conducted by Paul Westhead and Marc Cowling at Warwick University Business School in late 1995. In total 427 responses were received out of 1000 requests. The response bias appears to be small. The sample covers the full range of geographical, sectoral and firm size distributions and the impact of motivations on performance can be traced over time. It also allows us to ignore the very distinct and unique problems surrounding start-up businesses. However, it does not include the self-employed and the specific issues involved in their general reluctance to grow.

Understanding what motivates business owners is fundamental to understanding why some grow and some do not. We are also able to find out whether owners and firms change their motivations over time. This is particularly important since having a lifestyle objective in the start-up and early years might not necessarily condemn such firms to a future of low or no growth.

Overall, the data shows that around 60 per cent of smaller firms have the desire to grow to some extent and that this proportion varies substantially across sectors. This figure is similar to that found by both the Cambridge and Aston studies mentioned in Chapter One. Additionally, profits are important for the majority, but not all, smaller businesses. Below, we set out the broad trends shown by the data and then explicitly test for a link between motivations and actual growth.

Motivations and different types of firm

Table 2.1 shows just how important maintaining business independence is to the vast majority of small business owners. This has potentially significant implications for growth, as it is unlikely that such firms will be willing, for example, to sell equity.[5] This means that any funds for expansion must be supplied either from the owner through reinvested profits or by raising debt capital. The desire for independence, however, varies across sectors, with construction firms being the most open minded and manufacturers the least.

Table 2.1 Objectives by industrial sector				
	Percentage of firms with stated objective of			
	Independence	*Lifestyle*	*Sales growth*	*Profit margins*
Agriculture	70	65	65	75
Manufacturing	78	44	81	70
Construction	62	70	43	71
Retail	73	65	62	82
Finance	65	63	58	75
Other services	68	55	65	71

A substantial proportion of firms also have an explicit lifestyle objective. This also varies considerably across sectors, peaking in construction at 70 per cent and troughing amongst manufacturers at only 44 per cent but we note that manufacturing firms are particularly highly growth-orientated, whilst construction firms are not.

The evidence in Table 2.2 suggests that personal objectives do not preclude growth objectives since quite high percentages of firms can hold either a lifestyle or independence orientation as well as a sales growth or profit motivation. This point illustrates the danger of presuming that just because a person is oriented towards lifestyle

Table 2.2 Firms with dual motivations (percentage of firms)

Motivation	Growth	Profit
Lifestyle	58.4	78.3
Independence	62.8	80.0

considerations, it also means that that company will not grow. Lifestyle companies defined as 'no growth' are actually a very specific group of firms.

The clear result overall is that softer motivations, in the main, do not preclude firms from pursuing harder economic objectives such as growth or profit.

Table 2.3 Objectives by firm size (micro under 10, small 10-49, medium, 50-249)

	Percentage of firms with stated objective of			
	Independence	Lifestyle	Sales growth	Profit margins
Micro	79	74	55	77
Small	63	58	65	77
Medium	68	60	56	74

Looking at the same data split by firm size (Table 2.3), we can see that the desire to remain independent and to have a lifestyle objective is extremely high in micro firms. Perhaps the most interesting group is the small firm category. They seem to be less independent and more likely to want to seek sales growth than either micro or medium-sized firms.

If we look at different firm ages, Table 2.4 shows that older businesses appear to be slightly more protective of their independence than young firms. By contrast, however, lifestyle objectives appear to diminish slightly over time. This might be indicative of a cultural shift as small business owners become more aware of the opportunities open to

Table 2.4 Objectives by age of firm

	Percentage of firms with stated objective of			
	Independence	Lifestyle	Sales growth	Profit margins
Young	66	67	56	79
Old	71	62	61	75

their business in the post-survival phase. The evidence on sales growth is consistent with this.

In Table 2.5 we can see that founding entrepreneurs are more likely to be lifestyle orientated and less likely to seek sales growth.

Table 2.6 shows that product innovators are substantially more likely to be motivated by profits than non-innovators. This finding is generally consistent with the desire to develop new, high value added products and create new and profitable niche markets.

Table 2.5 Objectives by ownership type

| | Percentage of firms with stated objective of | | | |
	Independence	Lifestyle	Sales growth	Profit margins
Founder	69	67	57	77
Non-founder	70	60	62	75

Table 2.6 Objectives of product innovators

| | Percentage of firms with stated objective of | | | |
	Independence	Lifestyle	Sales growth	Profit margins
Innovation	68	62	65	81
Non-innovation	71	65	63	69

The research also gives support to the following conclusions:

- The smallest micro firms are by far the least likely to introduce product innovations.

- Younger firms who have grown are the most likely to be a source of innovation by seeking to develop and introduce new products.

- Firms still controlled by the founding entrepreneur are less likely to product-innovate, suggesting that ownership transfer or expansion may be a key issue.

- Process innovators and networkers both have a higher probability of being product innovators. The effect was very substantial for networkers, suggesting positive gains to innovative activity from networking.

The creation of networks amongst small firms and between small and large firms is currently the focal point for small business policy in many

OECD countries. Here we question whether firms currently involved in networking activities have identifiably different motivations and objectives from those who are not actively involved in networks. From Table 2.7 we can see that networking firms are less likely to have a strong desire to maintain their independence.

Table 2.7 Objectives of networking firms				
	Percentage of firms with stated objective of			
	Independence	*Lifestyle*	*Sales growth*	*Profit margins*
Networkers	63	64	63	74
Non-networkers	71	63	59	77

In total, one in five of firms in the sample are actively involved in networking activities. The results show that sector is an important factor in determining who networks, as is geographical location. Manufacturers are the least likely to be networked and other services, finance related and agricultural firms the most likely. In comparison with all other locations, firms in Yorkshire and Humberside and the South West of England are substantially less likely to network. Finally we note that product innovators are more likely to be networked.

What about actual growth and performance?

Here we use three basic measures of performance – sales growth, profit margins and employment growth – to see how the firms actually behave. We can also identify how many firms within each category could be classified as high growth over a three-year period using a standard definition of 50 per cent minimum sales turnover growth over the three years (NUTEK, 1998).

A key result from Table 2.8 is that growing firms generate substantially higher margins than non-growers. This is strong evidence to suggest that growth is positively related to profitability and by implication a desirable outcome for firms, particularly if profitability reflects increased efficiency. There are also substantial differences between sectors with, for example, retailers working on relatively low margins. Other important findings are that product and process innovators record higher profit margins.

The results are mixed on size and age. On profits, younger and

Table 2.8 Actual growth by firm characteristics

	Profit margin	Actual employment growth	Actual sales growth	% real sales growth	% job growth	% of high growth firms
Agriculture	14.23	1.6	0.68	52.7	16.8	40
Manufacturing	5.75	4.8	0.50	18.8	0.2	34
Construction	13.28	1.8	1.80	58.9	15.7	35
Retail	4.85	2.6	0.48	36.2	20.0	39
Financial	8.69	6.5	0.38	56.8	25.2	30
Other services	6.75	27.1	0.65	43.2	32.1	42
Micro	10.14	-0.5	0.21	29.3	0.8	30
Small	7.02	1.6	0.42	56.7	27.3	39
Medium	6.24	28.8	1.00	40.8	36.6	44
Younger	10.12	5.3	0.46	55.3	28.4	38
Older	7.20	5.5	0.44	42.1	17.4	37
Founder	9.72	3.9	0.36	46.3	22.3	37
Non-founder	6.54	6.6	0.51	44.4	18.3	37
Product-innovator	8.20	6.4	0.48	50.9	26.9	38
Non-innovator	7.42	4.0	0.40	36.9	10.0	35
Process-innovator	8.55	5.0	0.37	53.9	23.0	41
Non-innovator	7.49	5.7	0.50	40.2	18.2	35
Networker	8.06	6.2	0.58	41.5	41.6	38
Not networked	7.83	5.2	0.42	46.1	14.8	37
Growing	10.12	20.4	0.65	143.8	54.4	-
Not growing	6.57	-0.9	0.03	5.7	2.1	-

smaller firms seem to be more profitable on average, although there is a lot of variation in performance. On sales growth we find that small firms achieve the best performance, nearly double that of micro firms. Younger firms were also found to perform better on sales growth and job generation. There appears to be a strong and positive relationship between firm size and job generation.

These results are consistent with the idea that firms which can expand beyond the micro stage in their formative years are the most likely to continue to generate jobs into the future. In short, growth begets growth.

Business Links have historically explicitly targeted firms that have already grown beyond the micro stage. This may only be effective as a short-term strategy since it excludes the very class of firms who need the greatest level of support to step onto the initial, early phase, growth trajectory. However, on the ground many support providers realise this issue and continue to provide appropriate support to micro firms. Enterprise agencies in particular focus on new businesses and micro-enterprises.

How do motivations relate to actual growth and profitability?

Lastly, we address the most important question of all: whether motivations of smaller business owners actually matter to real outcomes for the company. Here we explicitly test for the effects of motivations on business performance using three measures:

- employment growth
- profits
- real sales growth

Table 2.9 The impact of motivations on business performance

Motivation	Employment growth	Profits	Sales growth
Independence	0	--	0
Lifestyle	(-)	0	0
Growth	+++	(+)	++
Profit	0	0	0

Notes: 0 indicates not significant, (+/-) indicates weak association, +/- indicates significant at 10% level, ++/-- indicates significant at 5% level, +++/--- indicates significant at 1% level.

The results in Table 2.9 clearly show that the desire for independence has no impact on sales growth, but reduces profits. This suggests that there is an economic price to pay for owners who are, for example, unwilling to open up their capital to outsiders. By contrast, a lifestyle orientation has no impact on profit or sales growth, and may only act as a minor constraint on job generation.

On growth and profit motivations, holding a profit objective, in reality, has no impact on actual realised growth or profit. This suggests that profits are, to a large extent, determined by a combination of firm characteristics such as age, size, industrial sector and geographical region alongside external macroeconomic forces over which the firm has little control.

Finally, by running a regression analysis of the data, owners with an explicit growth objective are 11 per cent more likely to achieve growth

---

Summary of findings from motivations study

Motivations
- Maintaining business independence is very important to the vast majority of small business owners but this varies across sectors. It is particularly high amongst micro firms.
- Lifestyle and independence objectives do not preclude growth since it is possible to hold growth objectives alongside these motivations.
- Small firms less likely than medium or micro to wish to be independent or to have a lifestyle orientation but more likely to seek sales growth.
- Lifestyle objectives appear to diminish slightly over time.
- Founding entrepreneurs seem to be less likely to product innovate, less likely to seek sales growth and more likely to be lifestyle oriented.
- Product and process innovators are much more strongly oriented towards growth.

Actual outcomes
- Growing firms generate substantially higher margins than non-growers
- Networkers and innovators also generate more profits, as do younger and smaller firms

Motivations and actual outcomes
- Owners of firms with explicit growth intentions are more likely to achieve actual growth.
- Desire for independence has no impact on sales growth but reduces profits
- Lifestyle orientation has no impact on profit or sales growth and only a minor constraint on job generation.
- Holding a profit objective has no impact on actual growth or profit.

---

holding all other things constant (for example, age, sector, size). In short, growth is, to some degree, dependent upon owners having the desire and willingness to grow. As such, we might conclude that the lack of growth in many SMEs is at least partly constrained by the anti-growth culture of their owners. By implication, our evidence also suggests that more firms could achieve growth should they take choose to re-orientate themselves.

For public policy-makers this both represents a problem and an opportunity. The problem is clearly that we have too many established micro firms who use relatively low level technology, are poor innovators and are inefficient. Further, they appear not to have the desire or motivation to grow, even if it were possible. Can interventions change growth orientations? We explore this further below.

Interventions can achieve changes in growth orientation

The recent Business Link Value for Money (VFM) study (PACEC, 1998) included a survey of growth orientations of Business Link users prior to

Table 2.10 Growth intentions of Business Link users prior to support

Type of support	% of firms with a rapid growth orientation
International trade/export	34.1
Events	30.8
Finance	30.2
Management training / hrm	27.0
Action planning	26.6
PBA (Personal Business Advisor)	24.8
Subsidised consultancy	23.6
Marketing	21.7
Innovation and technology	21.2

and after the use of Business Link services together with their actual growth. The analysis threw up some very interesting conclusions. We undertook further exploration of the data to determine just what the effects were.

We begin by considering how many SMEs were oriented towards rapid growth prior to receiving BL support. (The researchers used no explicit definition of growth in their questions to owner-managers.)

The basic data in Table 2.10 is informative as it sheds more light on the support areas in which potentially rapid growth firms are seeking advice. At the top of the list is international trade and exporting. This suggests that it is an area perceived by SMEs to be one in which the barriers to rapid growth are high. Other critical areas are events and finance. Events are associated with expanding the customer base and developing new markets.

At an industry level, substantially more firms in transport and communications and real estate held rapid growth intentions before receiving BL support (30.2 per cent and 27.1 per cent respectively). The sectors with the lowest proportions of rapid growth orientated firms were manufacturing and construction both with 18.3 per cent of firms. There was also evidence that firms with limited liability status were more likely to hold rapid growth intentions than all other legal types of firm.

Perhaps the most interesting finding concerns the company age. Here the evidence strongly supports the notion that younger firms are more orientated towards rapid growth. For example, the average age of firms reporting a rapid growth intention was 17 years compared to 35 years for firms seeking to reduce their size or 26 years for firms wishing to stay the same. The distinguishing feature between those with moderate growth intentions and those with rapid growth intentions was that the rapid growers needed to grow in order to increase their labour and capital productivity to reach comparable levels to those with moderate growth intentions. In other words, the rapid growers were initially less efficient than the others so that they had to grow rapidly to become equally or more efficient. Generally, as efficiency rises, so does profitability.

An important fact emerging from the data is that the 'rapid growth' orientated firms were remarkably similar in their characteristics to the 'stay the same' group, with the exception of age. The average turnover for the two groups was £2.8 million for the 'stay the same' group and £2.7 million for the 'rapid growth' group. Net assets were £0.47 million for both groups, and average employment slightly higher for rapid growers at 44 compared to 36. Although profitability was slightly higher in the 'stay the same' group, both labour and capital productivity was lower. This suggests that the decision not to grow is a deliberate choice taken by owners that may result in missed opportunities for growth, in the sense that growth could have been achieved had the owners been more orientated towards it.

Changing motivations

There is substantial evidence that, although growth orientations are not specifically targeted in most Business Link interventions, some firms in receipt of support subsequently re-orientate their growth intentions.

The basic data in Table 2.11 shows that relatively few SMEs have no growth orientation at all (but this sample is, of course, not random and there will clearly be a bias towards more growth oriented firms

Table 2.11 Future growth intentions measured after three years (percentage of firms)

Initial growth intentions	Subsequent growth intentions				
	Go smaller	Stay same	Moderate growth	Rapid growth	Total (%)
Go smaller	15.6	22.1	57.1	5.2	7.1
Stay same	1.3	48.9	46.4	3.4	21.7
Moderate growth	0.2	7.5	84.8	7.5	50.3
Rapid growth	0.4	1.8	22.5	75.3	20.9
Total (%)	1.6	16.3	61.5	20.6	100.0

approaching a Business Link). Of the remainder, only 21 per cent sought to grow rapidly, the rest seeking only moderate growth. Over the next three years, however, after receiving BL support, there was a significant upward shift in firms' growth intentions. In aggregate, a higher proportion of firms are orientated towards moderate growth, and fewer towards downsizing or stability.

When we consider these transitions at a more disaggregated level, even more interesting results appear:

- 62 per cent of firms which initially sought to downsize subsequently had a growth orientation, and within this group 5 per cent were looking to grow rapidly. This is perhaps the most dramatic transition.

- For firms which initially targeted stability, there was a fairly equal split in future growth orientation between those still focusing on stability and those focusing on growth.

- The numerically dominant group is those with moderate growth intentions in the initial period. Of these, nearly 85 per cent are still orientated towards moderate growth in the future but 7.5 per cent had stepped up their growth orientation from moderate to rapid growth. Only 7.5 per cent sought to stabilise their firms by downgrading their objectives from moderate growth to 'stay the same'.

- For those who focused initially on rapid growth, 75 per cent still have the desire for rapid growth. Furthermore, an additional 22 per cent still sought more moderate growth. Only a small proportion of initially rapid growth orientated firms sought future stability or downsizing.

On balance, this sort of evidence suggests that Business Link interventions, regardless of their impact in the short-term, have a strong impact on the cultural orientation of SME owners. If we then link this to our earlier evidence which showed that growth orientation has a decisive impact on actual realised growth, a fact confirmed by the PACEC (1998) report on BL users, then we might conclude that the long-term effects of BL activity can only be beneficial for many firms.

How do motivations impact on actual growth outcomes?

To identify the specific impact of motivations and the type of BL support given to firms, a growth equation was estimated which incorporated the four growth orientations and the nine different support interventions, alongside a host of other standard firm characteristics. The discussion below isolates the impact of the growth orientation and type of support on growth holding all other things constant.

If we consider four firms with otherwise identical characteristics, other than their growth orientation and in receipt of the same type of BL support, then the firm with the desire to stay the same size will generate 14 more jobs than the firm seeking to downsize. The gap expands if we consider firms with moderate or rapid growth intentions. Here the moderate growth orientated firm will create a further eight jobs than the 'stay the same' firm and the rapid growth orientated firm an additional 17 jobs on top of the moderate grower. Using turnover as our growth measure, the rapid growth orientated firm will increase its sales by two million pounds over and above that achieved by the rest.

The most successful interventions appear to be in the areas of management training and human resource management (HRM) and diagnostics (tools enabling firms to recognise their support and business needs). Both made significant contributions to growth over and above that achieved by other types of BL intervention. These findings are supported by West and Patterson (1999) who argue that employee's satisfaction with their work and a positive view of the organisation, alongside sophisticated people management practices are the most important predictors of the future productivity of companies.

What are the implications?

The evidence presented has established a strong link between initial growth intentions, BL intervention, actual growth and future re-orientation towards growth. This suggests that for a substantial number of SMEs the major barrier is their own lack of orientation towards growth. Thus one positive outcome of BL intervention is that it helps break down these cultural barriers. In policy terms, and setting aside the direct economic effects of BL intervention, our findings suggest that any mechanism by which policy-makers can effect such a cultural shift is worthy of consideration.

The economic value of BL intervention can now be characterised as the sum total of the cultural orientation of the firms receiving support plus the actual effects of the support received. In a dynamic sense, and having effected this cultural change, BL intervention has created a virtuous circle of future growth by boosting the numbers of firms with stronger growth orientations and by strengthening their ability to manage future growth. In combination, these two effects acting together are likely to enhance the desired and actual future growth of these SMEs.

Summary of results from Business Link survey

- Younger firms are more oriented towards rapid growth.
- Rapid growth firms were remarkably similar in their characteristics to companies who wanted to stay the same size indicating that growth is a deliberate choice.
- Business Link interventions can create an upward shift in growth orientations.
- The effect was most dramatic for those who had wanted to downsize, 62 per cent of whom now wanted to grow.
- The economic value of BL intervention can now be characterised as the sum total of the cultural orientation of the firms receiving support plus the actual effects of the support received.

We will look further at some of the impacts of Business Link services in the next chapter. But presented below are some schemes which are aimed specifically at changing orientations. Most are provided by Enterprise Agencies and hence are targeted at micro-enterprises, predominantly those companies most in need of support to effect cultural changes in attitudes to growth.

Case studies of innovative schemes

Business Development Programme – Business Enterprise Support Ltd

This programme was developed to address two major concerns that the team believed were significant constraints upon SME growth. The first was that owner-managers manage and operate their businesses in isolation, having very little contact with other SMEs or business networks. The second constraint was that SMEs very rarely develop business plans or financial forecasts, hence they effectively do not set explicit goals or targets for future performance. Many companies just drift aimlessly along in a very passive way.

The aim of the business development programme is to develop peer group networks of SMEs as a means of providing a focal point for shared experience, exchanges of skills and information, and ultimately facilitating growth. The programme seeks to identify 12 owner-managers of businesses with less than 50 employees. An important criterion is that none must be in direct competition with one another. The key role for the programme team is to act as facilitators. This entails maintaining group solidarity, encouraging, motivating and providing general administrative support. Crucially, the group itself agrees its own constitution, and sets individual and group targets. The group then works as a team towards these goals.

One of the more interesting features of the programme is the fact that the group collectively agree to make a cash contribution (identical for each firm) to a central fund which is then matched by challenge funding. This fund is then used to support the achievement of targets. Firms wishing to secure funds have to make a bid to the group, which is then either supported or rejected.

Looking at the bottom line, the original twelve firms (average size of firm is 5–12 employees) on the programme increased their combined turnover by £1.28 million, creating an additional 15 jobs and safeguarding a further four jobs.

The innovation of the programme lies in the use of groups of owner-managers of SMEs to promote self-learning. The role of the programme team is essentially to provide an environment conducive to this mode of learning. A measure of the success of the initiative is that it has been rolled out to other areas and expanded. The role of peer groups in helping businesses focus on growth and re-orientate themselves in terms of setting objectives and explicitly adopting strategies to achieve them, is one example of how culture can be changed with the right environment and level of support.

Objective 4 Programme – Chester-Le-Street Enterprise Agency.

The inspiration for this programme came from a realisation that two basic barriers were preventing smaller businesses from growing: the first was that skills deficiencies were not being identified by owner-managers; the second was that traditional methods of support, for example, training needs analysis, do not work because of time constraints on the owners. The new approach was to suggest to business that they should allow their customers to identify 'gaps' and 'needs'. In short, if you want to know what is right and wrong with your business, ask the customers. This has the added advantage of being more attractive to firms since it is a business-led relationship facilitated by the Enterprise Agency.

The actual process is quite simple. The programme manager identifies businesses from the EA portfolio, developed over its 15 year existence, who would benefit most. They are then approached on a one-to-one basis with a view to developing an appropriate survey instrument to identify customers' views of their business. This is where the owner-manager and marketing expert establish a close relationship. Having identified the customer base, drawn up a survey questionnaire and adopted the best means possible for eliciting responses, a fairly large-scale survey is then conducted. The returns are then collated and analysed and a report is written which includes recommendations for implementing the changes identified by the clients' business customers. It is also validated by one of the surveyed customers.

The EA team and the owner-manager then meet to help turn the recommendations into actions. Typically, the number of actions is less than ten, ranging from direct action, dealing with operational issues, to longer-term training needs such as attending a computer course or developing personnel skills.

The key factors which make this programme successful are:

- The extensive history of the enterprise agency as a local support provider, and particularly its historical focus on start-ups, means that probably an absolute majority of small business in the area have passed through its doors over the last fifteen years. Its client list is comprehensive and it does not waste time seeking out businesses to support. Matching businesses to programmes is done in-house through its historical client portfolio. For Business Links, this sort of matching would be very difficult. Furthermore, extensive resources are often wasted by Business Links on the identification process and/or marketing of support (see next chapter).

- The team strongly believe that its success is based upon the continuity of staff at the EA and the building up of relationships with businesses from pre-start stage to maturity.

- In addition, the delivery mechanism must be seen by the businesses to have a direct and tangible benefit.

- There must also be an element of knowledge transfer so that owner-managers are capable of replicating the exercise in the future.

- Ownership of the results gives the business a real commitment to change.

Example 1: a high-quality, garden furniture manufacturer.

The owner is, in many ways, the classic small businessman. He exercises very strong control rights over the business, yet is extremely wary of growth, viewing it as a threat, not an opportunity. In typical style, business was ticking over at a manageable and steady rate, but there were three problems. The first was that the business had a high turnover of operational staff. The second was that the mode of production was inefficient as phase two (the varnishing) had to shut down if phase one (the machining) was in progress because of limited floor space. The business needed further capacity to separate out the different phases of production.

The third problem was that the furniture's life-span was too long to develop repeat custom, therefore all the goodwill on the part of the customer was lost after the first, and only, transaction. After a customer survey, it became apparent that the mode of production was causing lengthy delays in delivery and that this was of great concern. Customers also identified a gap in the service provision. Many customers, for example, ended up re-varnishing the furniture themselves and found this to be unsatisfactory since they lacked the skills and knowledge to deal with high quality timber. The gap was therefore in after sales maintenance of the furniture.

On the basis of the customer survey and personal contact with the owner-manager, a change implementation strategy was formulated. This entailed several actions, the first of which was to buy some additional land and extend the existing premises to accommodate the two phases of production. The second was to develop the new care and maintenance service. Thirdly, the owner-manager is looking at Investors in People as a means of developing his personnel management skills in order to improve staff retention. This business has now very substantially increased its turnover.

Example 2: an abseiling window cleaner.

Essentially this unique service was having difficulty attracting customers. The EA team adopted a two phase strategy. In phase one the marketing expert arranged for a press release in the local media. Phase two consisted of compiling an address list with contact names for all suitable buildings within the geographical area. This business now has a number of new, long-term contracts at very little cost to itself and relatively low level, but critical, intervention on the part of the EA team.

ELIMINATE – Groundwork (Business Link East Lancashire)

The East Lancashire Waste Minimisation Club is a demonstration project involving waste audits, workshop sessions and developing waste minimisation opportunities. The project was set up in partnership with the East Lancashire Business Environment Network, the Environment Agency, Government Office North West, Environmental Best Practice Programme, AEA Technology, Northern Technologies, local SRBs and Blackburn City Challenge. To date 21 companies have been associated with Eliminate. The objectives are summarised below:

- to demonstrate the concept and benefits of waste minimisation within networks of participating companies.

- to achieve specified environmental impact reductions.

- to achieve specified financial and economic development targets.

- to evaluate and disseminate best practice from the project to assist other local firms to adopt waste minimisation policies.

The main barrier to the adoption of waste minimisation policies by SMEs was a cultural one in the sense that they didn't typically view waste minimisation as achievable or as a means of improving their bottom line. Owners and managers did not view waste management as an area on which to spend resources and time. The team, comprised of a scientist, supported by a graduate environmentalist, had to work very hard to convince SMEs that waste minimisation was worthwhile. Figure 2.1 outlines the process by which the team attracts firms onto their programme. What it does not show is the number of visits and seminars it takes to generate a firm commitment to the programme. The important point is that, for schemes seeking to alter individual perceptions and break down cultural barriers, the set up costs can be

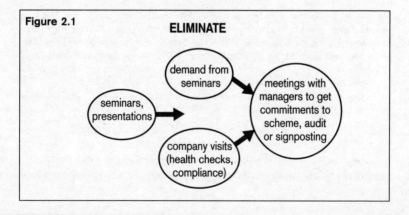

Figure 2.1

ELIMINATE

demand from seminars

seminars, presentations

company visits (health checks, compliance)

meetings with managers to get commitments to scheme, audit or signposting

large. Furthermore, there needs to be a long-term commitment to supporting this type of programme in order to achieve positive results.

The firms involved cover a wide range of industrial sectors including textile, paper, medical, chemicals and mechanical engineering. To participate, each firm has to pay a £1,000 subscription fee and commit to a minimum of 125 hours of staff time. In return, they receive a series of monthly workshops in which the management team are trained in the concepts and benefits of waste minimisation. In addition the Groundwork team regularly visit participant firms to provide training and advice to help implement specific initiatives which come out of the initial workshop sessions.

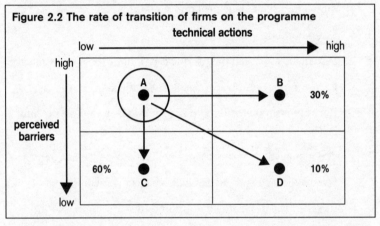

Figure 2.2 The rate of transition of firms on the programme

Figure 2.2 shows the rate of transition achieved by firms on the programme. The majority of firms begin in segment (A) where there are perceived to be very high barriers to adopting waste minimisation policies and relatively low, if any, degree of actions to address this issue. The programme's goal is to shift all participants to segment (D) where they have broken down the cultural barriers and adopted significant technical actions to promote waste minimisation. In reality this is clearly a difficult task, with only ten per cent of firms starting in segment (A) effecting the transition to (D). Yet the figure shows two things; firstly that with carefully designed programmes of support, perceived or cultural barriers can be broken down, and; secondly, even if those cultural barriers still remain, in a substantial number of cases firms can be persuaded to implement technical actions to reduce waste.

The programme has clearly delivered tangible benefits to its participants. For example, the average company has reduced the amount of waste going to landfill by eight per cent, reduced water usage by nine per cent and increased energy efficiency by four per cent. These are not trivial numbers in both an environmental sense and in terms of generating cost savings for the firms. In fact the average saving per firm is £135,000 per annum, effectively bottom line profit. For every pound spent on training, the programme has produced an average return of £35 in additional profit.

The team attribute the success of ELIMINATE to ten critical factors;

1   Commitment from managers who then provide a clear lead

2   Motivation of management and workforce

3   Team building

4   Systematic approach to introduction of basic tools and strategies

5   Focus on opportunities and simple solutions

6   Record and monitor data to use as evidence to convince future firms

7   Tell managers the exact cost of inefficient waste management

8   Feedback success to encourage managers and employees

9   Perseverance in identifying opportunities for minimisation

10   Talk to suppliers and customers about what you are trying to do

It is clear that a commitment to change people's perceptions and culture are the key to success. This approach has to be backed up by credible evidence concerning the economic impacts to the firm which not only helps maintain and stimulate the interest of participating firms but also acts as a demonstration to others.

Business Growth Programme – Centre for Small and Medium-sized Enterprises

Warwick Business School has been running this programme for several years. It is designed specifically for owner-managers of SMEs – generally micro-enterprises or slightly larger businesses. The focus of the programme is to develop the personal capabilities of the owner-managers and then adopt a growth plan that is then validated throughout the ten month training programme. The programme incorporates twelve participative workshops, one-to-one counselling, a business health check and a growth project. In line with other support programmes, the focus is very much on facilitating networking and shared problem solving. This is backed up by a high degree of business specific technical support.

Participants report both hard and soft benefits. For example, a substantial number of owner-managers report efficiency improvements averaging around 20 per cent. Furthermore, additional growth of about 20 per cent was reported over and above that which would have been achieved without the programme. Owner-managers also state that the major benefits came from developing networks, team building within their own businesses and improved management systems. They also report being more open to change and new ideas, and have increased confidence in their own abilities to manage growth.[6]

Conclusions

This chapter has shown quite conclusively that whilst maintaining business independence is very important to most small businesses – particularly micro-enterprises – lifestyle and independence objectives do not necessarily preclude growth. Small firms seem more likely to wish to open up their firms to outside support and seek growth than micro-enterprises or medium-sized companies.

These motivations have several impacts on actual performance. Those companies that are oriented to growth are more likely to achieve actual growth while those that seek profitability directly do not necessarily achieve it. The desire for independence appears to have no impact on sales growth but significantly reduces profits suggesting that not taking on outside expertise or capital has constrained their profitability. But a lifestyle orientation appears to have no impact on profit or sales growth. These results suggest that actual growth can be strongly affected by a growth orientation but is not significantly affected by lifestyle considerations or independence.

Policy needs to consider how it might encourage more micro firms to get on the ladder of sustainability and how to encourage more medium sized firms to seek continued growth. Some of the case studies presented show that it is possible to change culture within companies and address growth.

Even interventions not aimed explicitly at changing growth orientations can have significant effects. The growth orientations of firms taking up Business Link services were found to increase on average as a result of the interventions. The effect was most marked for those that had originally wanted to downsize. It was also virtually impossible to distinguish between those companies that wanted rapid growth and those that did not. However, those desiring rapid growth created more jobs and markedly increased their turnover.

These examples and analysis illustrate that it is possible to encourage and support more people to aim for growth. Potentially it could be possible to increase the number of high growth companies as well as enable more micro-enterprises to gain the capabilities to become sustainable and, for at least some, to encourage them to grow.

3. Business support and growth

Introduction

At the end of the last chapter, we noted the surprising impact of Business Link interventions on growth orientations. As part of the research for this report, we conducted a further survey of Business Links to look at the impacts of their services on promoting growth. Unfortunately, most Business Links were unable to provide us with the impact data that we required but, despite the small sample size, some interesting results arose out of the work.

Here we review the reasons behind the setting up of Business Links and some recent discussions of their performance. We then set out the results of our survey into Business Link activities and draw out the implications for current practice and for the future development of the Small Business Service.

Existing reviews of Business Link support

Business Links were intended to build longer-term relationships with clients and to be more responsive to their needs than previous suppliers of SME advice and support. They have sought to do this in two main ways. First, through the provision of Personal Business Advisors (PBAs), who aim to develop a long-term relationship with a portfolio of local businesses and provide independent advice tailored to their particular needs, and second, by developing sophisticated information systems to supply them with accurate and regularly updated databases of all SMEs in their local area. A recent Business Link (BL) evaluation concluded that:

> Business Links have had the effect of transforming a previously patchy and piecemeal pattern of provision into what is now a more-or-less universally available menu of defined services. (PACEC, 1998)

In their 1996 *Evaluation of Business Links*, Ernst and Young developed three basic typologies which highlight the differences in the ways such partnerships have developed on the ground. These are:

- Loose strategic partnerships – the overall strategy is shared, but the overall integration of services is not.

- Integrated service delivery – partner organisations maintain strategic autonomy, but co-operate at the operational level.

- Fully-integrated partnerships – both strategic decision-making and service delivery is fully integrated through, for example, joint-locations and employee-sharing arrangements.

The report implied that the transition from loose strategic partnerships to fully integrated partnerships was simply a question of stage of development, with more established BLs more likely to have reached the level of partnership integration. Ernst and Young (1996) identified five major barriers to partnership and service development:

- Concern by partners about the transfer of services to BLs and loss of brand image and revenue.

- Problems in BLs marketing to the target group of firms in the 10-200 employee range with growth potential.

- Uncertainty with regard to the government's commitment to the BL concept.

- Uncertainty over the direction of BLs and the role of different partner organisations.

- Technical problems, for example, service integration, dual branding.

Two core organisational forms have emerged through the BL network. The centralised model is characterised by a single site where all BL staff and sub-contractors are located. This typically involves a BL, Chamber of Commerce and/or TEC partnership, the so-called 'Super Chamber' creating powerful integrated organisations with combined memberships well above the national average for traditional chambers of commerce (Wylie, 1996). BLs may also offer increased accountability to the business community through the introduction of membership schemes. The 'hub and spoke' model has a central BL office surrounded by a series of 'spoke' offices which service well defined local areas. The number of spokes is defined by local business geography and political sensitivities.

Personal Business Advisors and BL counsellors

Personal Business Advisors (PBAs), Innovation Technology Counsellors (ITCs) and Design Counsellors (DCs) form the basis of BL services. In particular, Personal Business Advisors are the contact point with businesses. However, in many BLs, Customer Service Advisors (CSAs) are employed to build up contacts with the local businesses. Where this is not the case, Personal Business Advisors operate with a large degree of autonomy in the sense that they identify businesses, market BL services and co-ordinate other service provision. A further complication is that Personal Business Advisors can either be directly employed or self-employed. The Business Review is a central function of their case activities – a structured interview with the business owner which is written up as a report. This initial review is generally free of charge or heavily subsidised.

The key question for government in its current review of business support and in its consultations on the development of the Small Business Service is: are the Business Links providing added value? A related question is, even if they are, is the establishment of BLs crowding out services already available to SMEs in a given locality? The evidence from Priest (1999) is mixed across the range of services provided. This however contrasts with the conclusions of PACEC (1998) who suggested that BLs have actually stimulated private sector business support provision.

However, a recent study by Bennett and Robson (1999) indicated that the Personal Business Advisor (presumed to be the key innovation of Business Links) and diagnostics (tools which enable firms to identify their needs and solutions) have low use levels and appear to add little to that offered by specialist advisers. One of their key findings is that if you compare Business Link users and non-users, it appears that the former are using Business Links as one of many sources of public advice. They appear to be lower users of private sector advisors. The authors' conclusions are that Business Links do not appear to be behaving as 'one-stop shops' providing all relevant needs, neither are they avoiding competition with the private sector. They appear to be holding on to businesses through low levels of referral of clients on to appropriate private sector service providers.

We argued in *The Entrepreneurial Society* for more of a 'first-stop shop' approach. In other words, Business Links should refer clients to the most appropriate source of advice and support be that public or private. In fact, this was the BL's original intention. The key point of concern here is that if the incentives on Business Links are still to retain clients and generate revenue, there may be a strong element of deadweight since many firms who could take advantage of private sector services are making use of subsidised Business Links. We have noted that more could be done to encourage smaller and micro-enterprises to seek growth; resources may currently be being misdirected to firms that need less subsidised support.

How do Business Links identify their clients?

Table 3.1 Methods used to identify growth firms	
Method	*Number of responses*
Specific assessment methods:	
analysis by personal business adviser	32
partner advice and/or referrals	15
General assessment methods:	
growth record and potential	14
external market research	12
database analysis	12
sector analysis and targeting	10
other methods	10
analytical tools	9
telephone questionnaire and telesales	8
target marketing and/or mail shots	6
networking with multipliers and/or incubators	6
potential for and/or interest in exporting	3
financial growth analysis and/or viability	3
expanding products and/or services	3
market share and/or diversification	3
promotional programmes and focused events	2
size of business	2
outgrown premises	2
media reporting	2
increase in productivity	2
investment in capital plant and/or external finance	2
Total number of responses	**158**
[multiple responses allowed]	
Source: Priest (1999)	

The evidence suggests that nine per cent of all firms use Business Links, and 19 per cent of the original target group of 10-199 employee firms (see Bennett and Robson, 1999). The key issue of encouraging more companies to seek advice and support has often been seen as a demand side problem with SMEs being particularly averse to external advice. We will explore this issue further below. Other concerns have been expressed about the perceived quality of advice. However, this neglects the effectiveness of the supply side. How do PBAs and CSAs generate business?

Table 3.1 suggests that the identification process is varied and to a large extent *ad hoc*. This is a cause of great concern for researchers who believe that this puts too much power in the hands of individuals to determine who gets access to public sector resources (see for example Bryson, 1997). The fact that less than 25 per cent of BLs use databases to identify growth firms suggests that they are not aware of existing, nationally available on-line company databases such as ONESOURCE, used in academia by researchers for the best part of a decade. Indeed there is no reason why business schools could not be linked up to BLs to provide such market information. There also seems to be a low level of commitment to basic marketing or promotional activities.

Sectoral bias?

We saw from earlier evidence (see Chapters 1 and 2) that growth is substantially determined by the sector in which a firm operates. Whilst manufacturers have the highest propensity to export – a desirable outcome for the UK economy – it is surprising to note in Table 3.2 that BL services are overwhelmingly dominated by manufacturers who in reality only represent around 8.7 per cent of the total stock of SMEs (source: DTI SME Statistics Unit).

Parker and Vickerstaff (1996), in their study of how successful TECs and LECs are in reaching SMEs, found that: 'within manufacturing there are more readily identifiable sectors when compared to services [and] there is a will for TECs and LECs to organise on this basis' (p257). On the positive side, however, BLs appear to be able to identify and support a high and disproportionate share of high technology firms. We look further at this bias in the next chapter.

Table 3.2 Sectoral focus of Business Links

Sector	Number of responses
Manufacturing	20
Engineering	13
Tourism and leisure	11
High technology	10
Printing, publishing and paper	5
Clothing and textiles	5
Food and drink	5
Others	5
Transport and distribution	4
Health care and biotechnology	4
Exporting	3
Building and construction	3
Media, advertising and marketing	3
Business services	3
Agriculture	2
Financial and professional services	1
Chemicals, rubber, plastics, fuel and energy	1
Furniture, upholstery, and household goods	1
Crafts	1
Total number of responses	**100**

Source: Priest (1999)

Types of services used

Figure 3.1 shows that the most popular service is exports, followed closely by training, general business advice and marketing. These are all areas in which SMEs are identifiably deficient.

Rather surprisingly firms still approach BLs for grant advice, despite the reduced significance of this type of support in the 1990s. Overall, however, the types of service demanded and supplied are precisely the areas in which SMEs are most in need of advice and counselling.

Our survey of BL activities

In the course of this project, we conducted an extensive postal and telephone survey of BL core activities using a standardised questionnaire. The survey covered issues such as numbers of SMEs using a particular type of support, their demographic characteristics

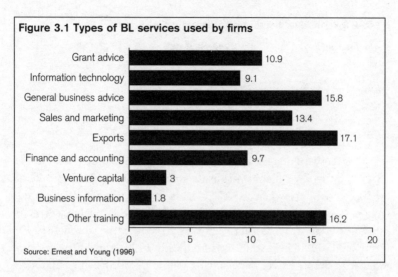

Figure 3.1 Types of BL services used by firms

Service	Value
Grant advice	10.9
Information technology	9.1
General business advice	15.8
Sales and marketing	13.4
Exports	17.1
Finance and accounting	9.7
Venture capital	3
Business information	1.8
Other training	16.2

Source: Ernest and Young (1996)

(size, age and sector), and a series of intermediate and final outcome measures. Of the BL respondents only 43 per cent were able to provide any final impact measures.

Due to the relatively low response rate to our survey, despite multiple recall, it is important to validate our sample against an existing sample of SMEs using BL support. However, the responses generated provide aggregate information covering in excess of 4,000 SMEs who recently used the BL network for support. We also have a balanced mix of design counselling, specialist manufacturing support, technology and export counselling activities. We opted to compare our sample against the most recent BL evaluation conducted by PACEC (1998).

Table 3.3 shows relatively few sample differences at the micro business end, but the PACEC survey reports larger numbers of medium sized firms receiving support. On a broad sectoral split, we can however see similar proportions of manufacturing firms accessing support (our survey 42 per cent – PACEC 46 per cent).

Table 3.3 The employment size distribution (percentage of firms)

Size	Our survey	PACEC
0-9	23	27
10-49	64	50
50+	13	23
Total	**100**	**100**

Table 3.4 The age distribution (percentage of firms)

Age (in years)	Our survey	PACEC
0-9	50	37
10-19	40	26
20-29	10	13
30+	0	24
Total	**100**	**100**

On age we find that there are fairly important differences (Table 3.4). Our survey suggests a considerably younger SME is typically in receipt of support, whereas PACEC finds one quarter of SMEs over the age of 30. These sample differences may reflect several issues. Perhaps the most important is that ours was conducted in summer 1999, compared to PACEC's which was from early 1998. Any differences may therefore simply reflect the changing nature of SMEs being supported through the BL network. A second critical issue is the year 2000 millenium bug. Younger and smaller firms are swamping BLs with requests for help with compliance issues. This effectively lowers the average age and size of firms supported.

On balance, however, we are fairly confident that the survey provides us with an up-to-date picture of current BL service provision.

Demand – supply of BL services

From our survey we find that the average support service deals with 193 approaches from SMEs per annum including the full range of service from basic desk/telephone enquiries to hands-on participatory support. Table 3.5 shows the average level of demand by broad category of support.

Table 3.5 Demand-supply of BL services

Type of support provided by BL	Number of firms per annum
Total	193
Design	95
Manufacturing	46
Technology	184
Other	565

Here we note that the provision of specialist support to manufacturers, for example the World Class Manufacturing Initiative, has the lowest provision. To a large extent this reflects the in-depth nature of support offered which is very time-intensive and costly to deliver. Basic telephone help-lines and desk based support have the highest level of provision, with the typical BL dealing with hundreds of enquiries per year. We might therefore conclude that our figures reflect both the demand from SMEs for BL services and the ability of BLs to fund particular services. From our telephone interviews with individuals, managing the more specialised support activities, we are led to believe that demand is higher than providers are able to supply given the current funding arrangements.

The demography of the firm

Here we present information covering the demographics of firm size and age for support recipients. The first point of note is that the median firm falls into the 10-49 employee size band and is between 10 and 19 years old. This suggests that BLs are, for the most part, reaching their currently defined target market. However, the remit of the Small Business Service is much wider including the self-employed and micro-enterprises so this is a comment only on the current state of affairs.

There are clearly substantial differences in the size of SMEs that are accessing each type of support service. For example, Table 3.6 shows that specialist manufacturing support is used by medium sized firms. All other services attract firms at the upper end of the small firm range. These results suggest two things: firstly, that smaller firms are unwilling to seek out support, and, secondly, that it is easier for service providers to identify and target larger sized SMEs. In either case, it appears that

---

Table 3.6 Employment size by type of support

Type of support	Average size of firm
Total	24
Design	21
Manufacturing	60
Technology	18
Exporting	18

Table 3.7 Age of firm by type of support	
Type of support	*Average age of firm (in years)*
Total	10
Design	9
Manufacturing	14
Technology	8
Exporting	9

there is a gap in the provision of support for the smallest of firms, arguably those most in need of support.

Table 3.7 shows that most firms receiving BL support are neither young nor mature. In fact it could be argued that they fall into the 'growth corridor' as predicted by life-cycle models and laid down in DTI guidelines. Certainly, firms of this age are unlikely to fail. If we match up the size and age figures, one fairly strong conclusion we can draw is that firms around ten years old, whose employment size exceeds the micro level by a considerable amount, have already achieved substantial growth. To this end support is being delivered to growth firms with presumably further potential to grow. Given our findings about past growth as a good indicator of future growth inclinations and ability, this is a consistent and rational intervention by BLs.

However, we are also wary of directing all support at firms that have already achieved growth for several reasons. Firstly, it may not be the case that enough firms achieve the required initial growth to attract the attention of BLs. Secondly, we question whether there is much 'value added' in supporting SMEs who have already demonstrated the ability to achieve unsupported growth. Should they not rather be offered appropriate signposting to private sector providers of services rather than be receiving subsidised support? Despite these concerns, it is likely that further growth for SMEs in this range would improve productive efficiency and substantially increase the likelihood of import substitution and exporting in the future.

Intermediate outcomes

So what is the value added of the actions that supported firms undertake? We looked at intermediate outcomes to try to find out exactly where the 'value' of the support is coming from. For example, if

Table 3.9 Intermediate outcomes	
Outcome	% of support initiatives
New Markets	77
New Products/Processes	83
Management Systems	77
Productive Efficiency	57
New Customers	63
Supply Chain	60
R&D	54

an owner-manager received support from a design counsellor what did he or she then do? We might expect that new designs might facilitate entry into new markets and an expansion of the customer base.

Table 3.9 suggests that BL intervention is focussed largely on helping businesses to develop new products/processes, new markets and improving their management control systems to support better planning. Less emphasis is placed upon enhancing productive efficiency in a direct fashion, or on developing new customers *per se*. However, it is likely that the secondary effects of developing the first set of areas will help achieve increases in efficiency or attract new customers. Indeed, to a large extent entry into new markets and/or the development of new products/processes is linked to improved management systems and better planning.

We also find that design counsellors appear more focused on providing an integrated package of support which encompasses new product/service development, backed by R&D, alongside improved management information and planning systems. In many cases this is also linked to accessing new markets. Technology counsellors appear more focused on improving productive and managerial efficiency in order to support new product/service development. By contrast, export counsellors tend to focus very explicitly on providing new products or services to new export markets.

Final outcomes

In order to address the final outcomes or the impacts of the whole process of policy intervention, we used three basic measures: employment growth; sales growth and profitability growth. Firms were asked how much actual growth was realised and of that what percentage

Table 3.10 Final outcomes
per cent growth arising from Business Link intervention on top of that which would have been achieved otherwise

Growth	% from base year	PACEC 1998 Survey
Employment	7.5	7.0
Sales	10.4	5.0
Profit	12.6	15.0

they believed was attributable to the Business Link support. A typical company stated that it would have only achieved 20-30 per cent of its actual growth in the absence of any intervention.

The evidence reported in Table 3.10 suggests that an average support intervention has been successful in helping SMEs to grow over and above that which they would have achieved in the absence of BL intervention. Indeed, the results are consistent across our three measures. It is also interesting to contrast them with the PACEC (1998) findings where a similar question was asked, although their results cover a three-year period from 1994 to 1997 which was also a time of different economic conditions. On balance we find two points of reassurance. Firstly, that our results are fairly consistent with those of a recent and large-scale BL evaluation, despite our focus on the support provider, rather than the firms, as the source of data. Second, the results overall are positive in the sense that policy intervention is making firms more profitable, and at the same time increasing sales and generating new jobs. But in general, support appears to improve profits and sales more than employment.

Survey conclusions

Our research shows that the way in which Business Links generate business is largely *ad hoc* and little use is made of existing online databases of companies.

●   The take-up of Business Link services is overwhelmingly dominated by manufacturing even though such firms only represent 8.7 per cent of the total stock of firms.

●   There seems to be more demand for high value-added interventions such as the World Class Manufacturing Initiative than there is supply.

- Business Links are attracting firms (or choosing firms) at the upper end of the small firm range which suggests that smaller companies are not seeking out support and also that it is easier for service providers to identify and target larger-sized SMEs. There is thus a gap in support for micro-enterprises which is currently only partially filled by the Enterprise Agencies.

- Most firms in receipt of support have already achieved growth and we question whether this approach ignores those firms that have not achieved sufficient growth to merit attention. We are also concerned that many established and growing firms could have been signposted to private sector providers rather than receiving subsidised support.

- Support interventions have succeeded in helping companies to grow beyond that which would have occurred otherwise. In general the support appears to improve profits and sales more than employment.

Implications for current Business Link practice

Evaluation

As a result of conducting the survey, we noted several inadequacies in the way in which outcomes of Business Link activities were measured:

- Less than half of the BL service providers were able to provide any final impact measures. This is surprising given the importance of such information for the ongoing development of programmes. The DTI Business Link Performance Assessment Unit has now introduced a requirement for business support agencies to provide impact figures and therefore this situation should be changing.

- Evaluation of SME initiatives seems to be more ad hoc, less systematic, and much more variable in quality than in many other countries. Techniques used by BLs range from so called 'happy face/sad face' methods to more sophisticated survey methods and statistical analysis. We realise that the business imperatives on BLs mean that they find it hard to find the time or money to undertake such work but it is important to have comparable rigorous data across BLs to enable future planning of appropriate support services. There is also great variation in the technical rigour applied to national evaluations, which range from the presentation of basic data to advanced econometric methods. Often this reflects the relative abilities of particular types of contractors to undertake detailed statistical analysis.

- Funds for evaluation are low when compared to the annual costs of many schemes and the potential benefits derived from proper evaluation. One recent, and large scale, evaluation in the UK had a budget which approximated to only 0.17 per cent of the annual costs of the scheme.

- Business Links have recently been equipped with Client Management Systems (CMSs) which are databases that track client details over time including the type of intervention they received and any changes in their performance. However, it is not clear that the BLs are using these systems effectively since many could not provide us with the data required to permit full evaluation of schemes. The proper use of the CMSs should substantially reduce the cost of evaluation and permit more real time, longitudinal impact studies.

Identifying and targeting firms

- The methods used to target firms are varied and to a large extent *ad hoc*.

- Less than 25 per cent of BLs use databases to identify growth firms. This suggests that they are not making full use of existing, national on-line company databases

The reliance on the Personal Business Advisor suggests that currently there is no clear approach to identifying firms which is based on good market data. The lack of localised, or national, registers of businesses means that resources are wasted in trying to identify firms would be likely to benefit from the provision of support.

It is likely that a more innovative and proactive approach to attracting new customers will encourage those firms who are the least likely to seek out advice and support and where the greatest impacts could be made. Methods of encouraging more firms to make use of services could involve increased links between the banks and accountants in order to encourage referrals and the use of business clubs and networks as ways of drawing more people into a culture of accessing external advice and support.

Who receives support?

- BL services are overwhelming dominated by manufacturers who only represent 8.7 per cent of the total stock of firms.

- There are substantial differences in which size of SME is accessing different services. For example, specialist manufacturing support is used by medium-sized firms. All other services attract firms at the upper end of the small firm scale. This implies that smaller firms may be unwilling to seek out support and that BLs find it easier to identify and target larger sized SMEs.

- Support tends to be delivered to firms which have already grown significantly and presumably have the potential to grow further.

There appears to be a gap in the provision of support for the smallest firms, who without intervention are never likely to expand beyond the micro stage. As we saw in the previous chapter, it is precisely those firms who could benefit considerably from innovative support.

Implications for the Small Business Service

While it is important to encourage as many firms as possible to seek external advice and support, it is not clear that the Business Link approach is appropriate for all companies. The research by Bennett and Robson (1999) indicated that the general services of the Personal Business Adviser were much less used by clients than more specific advice from counsellors suggesting that those who accessed support already knew what they wanted.

Catalysing flexible market-oriented networks of advice and support

The research in the next chapter indicates that embedding support more firmly within sectors may have a strong impact in encouraging more owner-managers to access appropriate advice and training. It is also very clear that future business support is going to have to be highly flexible and responsive to rapidly changing markets and business models. For that reason it is appropriate to locate more of it within peer group networks and within the realities of markets. This should result in increased relevance and numbers of access possibilities for companies. The use of new technologies will enable this process but, as our seminars demonstrated, the key is to increase understanding of different small firm needs and increase dialogue between all relevant groups so that solutions can be found. Support agencies and government will need flexible and pump-priming finance to be able to play a catalytic role and help create innovative and appropriate solutions.

Both the Small Business Service and the Regional Development Agencies will also need the capability and capacity to create networks between support providers (whether public and private) and therefore create synergies between them again allowing for more points of access for individuals to relevant support. It is not clear yet that they have the remit or flexibility in terms of resources to engage in enough of such activity even though some of the RDAs have begun to set out ways to rationalise and network the business support within their area and create public-private partnerships to tackle specific issues.

Engaging the micro-enterprises

If we look at an example of a recent survey of where small firm owner-managers go for advice, we find that of 30 per cent who sought external advice, 45 per cent looked to accountants, 26 per cent to banks and 16 per cent to solicitors (Office World, 1994). Advice from government agencies, consultants and business organisations was less important. Different surveys give different rankings but although there has been an increase in Business Link use over the last few years, it is vital to recognise the role of banks and accountants as first ports of call. Other companies will go to their trade associations, local authorities, enterprise agencies, private sector consultants or seek out specific sectoral support.

These comments illustrate that there is no one way to engage firms. The proposed Small Business Service aims to deal with a much wider range of firms by utilising as far as possible new technologies to deliver advice and a call centre to answer questions and direct companies on to sources of advice. The danger here is that the artificial distinction between growth and lifestyle companies may be reinforced and Business Link added-value services will actually be delivered to those who could have got their advice from elsewhere.

As the examples in Chapter 2 illustrate, there are cost-effective ways of addressing business development in more than one company at a time – for example, through self-help networks, business clubs – and many TECs, Links and Enterprise Agencies have experimented with such initiatives. Scottish Enterprise provides another model of engaging people through its Personal Enterprise Shows that travel the country encouraging people to consider starting up businesses (Gavron *et al*, 1998). Encouraging sectoral initiatives and local networks will provide other opportunities to spread knowledge and transferable skills. In this way, more headway can be made in reaching the 'hardest to reach' companies.

Increasing small firm voice

The DTI has said that the Small Business Service will listen more to small firms. In order to reflect on the diversity of small firms and to access the views of the self-employed and micro-enterprises who are under-represented by existing lobby groups or trade associations, it will be necessary to ensure that a large number of groups are represented and consulted. This may mean creating new interest groups and accessing underrepresented small firms through surveys and focus groups at the national, regional and local level.

Ensuring local flexibility

Local flexibility is critical to engaging business and providing appropriate services. (Jari *et al*, 1999) argue that in Ireland, a more bottom-up approach to small firm policy involving greater links with local interest groups and greater local design (alongside more sectoral and targetted support) has resulted in increased take-up of services. The authors argue that:

UK local support agencies in particular have traditionally offered 'top down' support. Programmes have typically been centrally determined and delivered in a standard form. This has made it more difficult for local SME owner-managers to see the programmes as meeting their specific needs.

Although there has been increased local flexibility, the proposed franchise approach to delivering the Small Business Service may break up existing critical partnerships which are necessary to identify appropriate needs and solutions. There is probably therefore a need to build on, or create where necessary, stable sub-regional strategic partnerships that involve all key players such as finance providers, local authorities, business representatives, and voluntary sector bodies which can cross-cut the business support, training and regeneration agendas. This type of public-private partnership will be further explored in the context of IPPR's Commission on Public-Private Partnerships which is due to report in early 2001.

4. Taking a sectoral approach

Introduction

As part of our research programme, we held a series of seminars that aimed to address the barriers to growth for small firms within three industries – printing, music and management consultancy. These sectors cover different types of industry but were not chosen to represent service, manufacturing or any other grouping of sectors. Rather the approach we took was to take the sectors as starting points in their own right and see to what extent sectoral differences or specific barriers might be relevant to any future development of business support. However, obvious difficulties arise straight away – sectors hide a multitude of subsectors, and sector boundaries are constantly shifting and changing. Indeed, you could argue that some of the most innovative companies in sectors often come from outside an industry or cross sector boundaries.

Policy support is currently focused on clusters, groups of interrelated firms that interact locally or regionally and who may be from a variety of industries. But it remains important to pay some attention to the sector because a key thread running through each of the seminars was that differences in industries matter because small growing firms are embedded within different types of markets. Growth can mean different things in different industries as can the way in which barriers to growth such as access to finance or advice and support are manifested. One way to work with these differences is to locate support as far as possible within sectors and within the links between firms, encouraging companies to build their capacity and respond to changes in market circumstances. In other words, the aim is to increase the capacity for self-help based on access to up-to-date knowledge of both markets and relevant support provision. The implication for the public sector is that its role changes from just being a direct service provider to also being a catalyst for action and for spreading information. That is not to say that generic support and direct provision of services are not appropriate and relevant – we saw how effective some Business Link provision has been – but there also needs to be recognition of the role of supporting flexible self-help responses.

A key challenge for the Small Business Service and for the Regional Development Agencies is to embed this awareness of the diversity of small firms into the analysis of the small firm sector and into support provision at a national, regional and local level. The Small Business Service also needs to proactively engage with the legislative process so that proposed policies are thoroughly tested out with small companies across sectors – beyond any simple exhortation to just 'think small'.

To understand and work with small firm diversity, there has to be widespread understanding of different business models, particularly amongst policy-makers, support providers and financiers. But there is surprisingly little literature in this area. What analysis there is has been commissioned as part of very practical responses to sectoral needs. As we saw in the first chapter, most academic research into barriers to growth for small firms has been based on manufacturing companies, and hence adopts a very specific view of growth. It was very clear from our discussions that it is critical to continually review the dynamics of sectors and the changing challenges and opportunities facing different sizes, structures, or growth orientations of firms. It was also apparent that there could be a great deal more activity that brings together all key players such as small companies, trade associations, government, finance and support providers and accountants in order to identify issues and attempt to provide appropriate practical responses. Even in the short meetings we held, ideas were aired, contacts made and some actions initiated.

Sectors and small firms

We have already explored the different growth orientations and needs of small businesses distinguished by, for example, size, or age. That analysis indicated the difficulties with any general small firm policy initiative which is not aware of and responsive to differing needs. But small firms also differ according to the type of industry in which they are found.

Indeed this fact is recognised in policies towards high-tech small firms, within DTI's Sector Challenge and particularly in the ways in which government departments sponsor different industries. There are also a whole host of sectoral initiatives, whether national networks or local support funded by a mix of government, industry or European funding. But the biggest problem about small companies is that most academic research has been generic and biased towards manufacturing, resulting in a model of growth and analysis of needs which might not be replicable elsewhere. Much less attention has been paid to the challenges and opportunities facing small firms across sectors and the differences between them. There is also some evidence that indicates that this bias is also reflected in some business support service providers. The financial community will also have different levels of sophistication in relation to their knowledge and expertise of different sectors although conversations, particularly with the banking community, indicate an increasing sophistication in understanding of industry risks and market conditions.

Ironically, although the recent Competitiveness White Paper (DTI, 1998) championed the knowledge driven economy, it seems as though it is those companies who epitomise the use of knowledge and creativity which are those that are the least understood and hence the least catered for. But there is increasing recognition of the need to understand and respond to these differences through, for example, the Creative Industries Taskforce or Biotech Means Business.

There is also a need to recognise that the complexity of sectors and subsectors may mean that they do not present a coherent face to public agencies and hence are not taken into account in policy-making compared with other more organised lobby groups. The recent EU White Paper on Commerce (CEC, 1999) made the point well with regard to retail. It stated that:

> [there is] the need to remedy the poor recognition of the sector by the public authorities at all levels, which is said to result in the sector's interests being ignored in debates on a variety of policies.' This stems in part from 'the extremely diversified nature of the enterprises within it, with their different market segments, business cultures and types of location, all of which make public presentation of their case difficult... The sector is affected by a large number of horizontal, national and European policies but often without its particular characteristics and needs being taken into account in the formulation of these policies.

So why might sectors matter?

The implications of taking a sectoral approach might well affect the way in which small firm policy is designed and delivered. We have only made a start in this area and in the time available for our research can only indicate some of the issues which need to be debated.

However, it is clear that some key questions include:

- To what extent are small firm barriers generic or sector specific?

- Does a sectoral approach to implementation make any difference to impact and outcomes?

- How do generic top-down small firm policies impact on sectors – are there different trade-offs?

Some examples of the importance of including a sectoral dimension to small firm policy-making and implementation are presented below:

Encouraging increased use of advice and support

We know that the take-up of advice and support by companies is low but that many finance and business support providers believe that this can be a crucial part of a company's ability to survive and grow. The key message from all the seminars was that there was generally very little financial awareness amongst the smallest firms and inadequacies in management skills and knowledge. But in Chapter 3 the PACEC survey of Business Links showed that take-up (and/or provision) of services is far higher amongst manufacturing firms than is reflected by their contribution to the economy. There could be several reasons behind this. For example:

- services are more tailored to manufacturing – those that fit the manufacturing model of business needs and growth better than for other sectors

- advisors understand manufacturing better than other industries

- manufacturing companies seek out advice and support more than other firms

- marketing is more towards manufacturing

- more manufacturing firms tend to be of the size and profile aimed for by Business Links since they tend to start out larger

It is as yet unclear which of these explanations might be the predominant one but it does appear from conversations with support providers and sector representatives that all of them are to some extent true. Evidence from the seminars suggests that some sectors do not perceive the available support as relevant to them. This was particularly true of music and management consultancy. There are, of course, examples around the country of TECs and Links who have set up sectoral networks and specific business support in recognition of differing needs. Portobello Business Centre in London is an example of an Enterprise Agency which has introduced sector networks and tailored modules in areas such as retail, fashion and music. It has found a very positive response to adopting this approach and is likely to extend it further. The rationale behind this initiative was that many people are talented individuals with creative and technical skills but do not have the equivalent understanding of business skills. It was felt that a sectoral approach would help in encouraging such people to take on advice and support.

There are other models of sector service delivery to small firms whether through trade associations, or via specific development agencies such as the Merseyside Music Development Agency. More research needs to be done to evaluate the effectiveness of these approaches and to ensure that as far as possible there are links between these different service providers in order to maximise the impact of interventions and to refer clients on to the most appropriate source of expertise. This might seem an obvious point to make but it is blatantly not happening on the ground.

An important part of many sectoral development agency and local network initiatives is that they can enable their members to respond very quickly to changing markets and provide people with the information and contacts to find business opportunities. They can encourage people to join together to find joint solutions and strategies as they arise, whether that is, for example, to access markets or create appropriate learning opportunities.

One example of the potential for this kind of activity is a group of Merseyside music companies (Merseyside Music Export Consortium, MMEC) who aim to market the region's music internationally through, for example, planning a joint marketing approach to MIDEM, the international music conference in Cannes in January 2000.

Such initiatives illustrate a critical role for the public sector in catalysing the formation of networks which create access for companies to appropriately designed advice and support and often to finance and opportunities for joint activities. Such networks may pull together existing provision, create signposts and clear access points. Examples of national networks are set out in the section on the music industry and in the Software Business Network described below.

> **The Software Business Network (SBN)** was formed in February 1998 with a three year DTI Sector Challenge Grant and several commercial sponsors. Fundamentally, the SBN is a self-help collaborative network which helps to create solutions to the needs of SMEs in the IT industry. Its aim is to 'accelerate the growth of SME software companies in the UK... We will achieve this by re-cycling the knowledge and successes of the IT industry and by delivering a set of products and services designed to have a positive and profound impact on growth and profitability.' They believe that the key will be to 'understand the SME's needs and to deliver relevant and timely solutions. We have established an SME growth model which identifies phases of growth and the specific business needs and success factors associated with each phase. Against this model we can benchmark performance and provide a set of relevant services either on a one-on-one basis through our mentor programme, or in groups, through our seminars.' Services include regional seminars, mentoring (including non-executive director support), facilitating venture capital provision and creating introductions to investors, business angel matching, valuating business propositions and technical support. SMEs can also interact through a website.

Would taking a sectoral approach alongside other provision increase take-up of external advice and support? Curran *et al* (1999) argue that in Ireland a far more sectoral and targeted approach (on the basis of characteristics such as firm size) has resulted in the increased take-up of advice and support by small firms. They argue, contrary to the prevalent UK thinking, that fragmentation and overlap of services is to some extent inevitable if you take a more bottom-up approach to small firm support. This method, however, creates many more relevant responses to needs therefore increasing the likelihood of companies taking advantage of the services provided.

Smallbone *et al* argue from their work on *The Characteristics and Strategies of High Growth SMEs* (1995) that:

It is important to recognise the sectoral context as a framework for considering the strategies associated with growth. It is a sector which defines the factor and technology choices, and often the opportunities for growth and the type of growth strategy, that are likely to be successful. This is reflected in the variations between sectors in the importance of product innovation to competitiveness and also in the type of investment strategy associated with successful growth performance... The importance of the sectoral context has implications for the provision and delivery of external advice and assistance to SMEs since sector-based support has a higher chance not only of being acceptable to clients but also of making a real impact on the business.

From an analysis of business support needs in the printing sector, Smallbone *et al*, (1997) set out the relative benefits of generic and specific expertise. While generic support may be fine for some businesspeople and particularly for start-up companies:

>...a common perception of many small firm owners is that what is needed is industry specific advice delivered by specialist consultants who understand their industry. The reality is that there are some areas where sector-specific assistance is essential (such as certain areas of technical assistance), others where it may be desirable (such as analysis of market trends or specific advice about suppliers), and others where it may not really be needed at all. However, on the basis that 'the customer is always right' and because of the reluctance of many small firm owners to look towards external assistance, an approach which understands and recognises the attitudes that are typical of small firm managers for sector-specific assistance is likely to be productive. In this context, the aim should be to develop a network of advisers and consultants with sector-specific knowledge and experience.

By so doing they argue that it might be possible to increase the demand for services overall.

Of course, as we noted in Chapter 3, most people seek out advice from a variety of outlets but most of these sources of information and advice will be generic. It is important to ensure that accountants, banks, and other access points for small businesses are aware of sectoral initiatives and can sign-post their customers on. The Small Business

Service potentially has a role here in creating, encouraging and catalysing sectoral networks and information links. As Andy Pratt of the LSE pointed out recently:[7]

> There is a role for a new type of policy maker who understands industries. With local policies there is a problem because reactive services need to be all-knowing and they do not address industries and the strategic nature of change. You need to build strategic knowledge and distribute this. The intervention is to make the networks work and fill the strategy gaps.

This is a clear example, of bottom-up flexible small firm policy.

Designing small firm policies and the impact of legislation on different companies

This is another area where the rhetoric of policy towards business and the reality of practical policy based on certain models of business and the economy conflict. There needs to be a great deal more research into industries outside traditional manufacturing and a realisation on the part of civil servants and policy makers that policies need to be tested out in a far more systematic matter than has been the case. This principle has been recognised in the recent Small Business Service consultation but only to the extent that legislation has to 'think small' – it should also think about different market conditions.

A recent example of the importance of understanding changing business models and of testing legislation out over sectors and different types of company is the now infamous Inland Revenue 35 – new rules introduced through the Finance Bill which amend the Welfare and Pensions Act. The idea behind IR35 is to reduce tax avoidance by preventing people from opting out of employed status (or being forced out of employment) and offering their services as independent self-employed through personal service companies. By doing so it is possible to avoid paying tax through paying yourself in dividends or storing profits and avoiding tax through a beneficial capital gains outcome. This situation also means that the previous employer does not have to pay national insurance.

Another obvious reason for wishing to clamp down on this type of activity is to protect employee rights. The extreme case is where employees are sacked and then forced to provide their services through a personal service company. The Unions have been vociferous in trying to make such practices illegal. Examples have been found, for example, in the construction industry. The Government believed that by introducing this legislation it would stop this abuse and at the same time recover lost revenue for the Treasury (Inland Revenue Press Release, 9 March, 1999).

> The proposed changes are aimed only at engagements with essential characteristics of employment. They should affect only those cases where these characteristics are disguised through use of an intermediary – such as a service company or partnership. There is no intention to redefine the existing boundary between employment and self-employment.

However, the strength of the backlash from different industries indicates the variety of effects such legislation might have on legitimate business models across a range of sectors. The managing director of one such affected company, Praxis Executive Taskforce, argued in the *Financial Times* (FT letter, 4 August 1999) that there is:

> the emergence of an independent executive workforce of interim managers and similar executive contract employees, prized for their ability wherever they go. They have forfeited employee rights and corporate perks for the challenge of independence.

Some of those risks are managed through personal service companies. Another example would be that of photographers operating through an agency which can feed work through. These are prime examples of knowledge-based workers using intermediaries as a way to gain access to market or to share resources in say marketing. In management consultancy a similar situation could arise when, for example, five members of a networking club bid together for a piece of work and work under the tradename of say a lead consultant (a virtual company). The current proposals might mean that the lead consultant then has to pay PAYE/NHI for the other consultants.

The IT industry has argued that such changes would alter the nature of self-employment and lead to a huge braindrain of specialists. One objector wrote in the *Telegraph* (7 June, 1999): 'The legislation effectively assumes that one-man companies are tax avoiders while larger companies are entrepreneurial. Yet Microsoft started with one employee.' The Institute of Chartered Accountants was quoted in the same article as saying that the 'application of these new rules will be aimed almost exclusively at inhibiting the growth of small businesses'.

The case of IR35 clearly illustrate the need to understand more fully the changing nature of business practices where outsourcing is used or where independent freelancers choose to come together to pool their ability to attract business through an intermediary. But at the same time it also highlights the very great difficulties of dealing with a situation which may be both a positive choice for some individuals (and of benefit to markets and growth) and one where people are just being exploited and where an employer is seeking to evade tax. The challenge for Government will be to find legislation that is capable of distinguishing between these scenarios and the shades of grey in-between.

Another example of the need to understand changing business models and the impact of intellectual property is the inapplicability of certain investment incentive schemes such as the Enterprise Investment Scheme (EIS) to those companies which have a percentage of their income derived from licence and royalty revenue. The EIS is an important tool to encourage the demand and supply of venture capital. It provides incentives in the form of tax relief to outside investors. But any company receiving at least 20 per cent of income from licences and royalties is exempt – except film companies.

The Inland Revenue takes the view that income from royalties is super-profit – not wealth creation. But in a world where knowledge, either embodied in people or in intellectual property, matters business plans incorporate the returns from exploitation of ideas as well as the direct sale of products and services. The old model of business economics being taken by the Treasury completely contradicts Government rhetoric supporting the knowledge-intensive industries. The music industry exemplifies another danger of such broad exemptions. Small independent record companies for the most part do not even reach the threshold of 20 per cent income from royalties. It is the larger companies who have a much higher proportion of their income derived from this kind of revenue stream and even that is falling with some companies now repatriating some of their licensing arrangements to the UK in preparation for changes to the industry arising from the Internet and digital trading.[8]

Implementation of small firm policies

Do policies have to be implemented in different ways to make them more effective? There is a tendency in the small firm policy arena to address broad issues with broad responses such as the Small Firms Loan Guarantee Scheme or the proposed regional 'equity gap' funds. But there are several reasons why some small firms cannot or do not access loan finance or equity, including issues relevant to different types of industry.

Knowledge of sectors can result in more appropriate and effective implementation of proposals. In the area of equity, the US recognises the importance of taking a sectoral approach through more industry specific finance instruments and expert advisors. In the UK, Scottish Enterprise has been looking at the development of sector specific equity funds (along the US model) to support their cluster strategies. The Software Business Network mentioned above has developed its own Business Angel Network. The music industry case study also points to a need for more industry-specific financial instruments to increase demand and supply for appropriate finance.

Conclusions and recommendations

Implications for national policy

- There is a need to rectify the bias towards manufacturing in academic and policy research.

- There is also a need to improve awareness of business models in different industries and ensure that business support recognises these and can respond accordingly.

- The Small Business Service must have the clout to be able to ensure that legislation is not only checked to see whether it has passed the 'think small' test but whether it has been adequately assessed for its impacts across the range of possible industry and business models. It therefore has to have real power in its relationships with other relevant departments, particularly the Treasury.

- The Small Business Service cannot just be concerned with the integration of national, regional and local delivery of generic services. There needs to be a huge change in understanding of how more people might be encouraged to use business services and to recognise that another way of drawing more people into a culture of accessing appropriate advice and support is through sectors. The Small Business Service must also be able to have the capacity (including flexible finance) to catalyse and pump-prime initiatives that draw together and maximise the effectiveness of both generic and sector-specific business support and to ensure that there are links between all providers. That flexibility should also be available to the Regional Development Agencies so that they are capable of realising their unique ability to create appropriate partnerships and synergies between support provision.

Implications for sectors

- There is a great deal more scope for self-help by different industries in conjunction with government, and finance and support providers, for example, with the creation of networks of information that draw together all relevant sources of advice and support. Such networks can investigate ways of encouraging people within sectors to put something back into the industry whether as mentors or business angels and to create the fora where relevant issues can be raised and tackled in an on-going way.

- Trade associations are variable in their attention to the needs of small business owners. There are ways in which they can work with and promote the development and greater awareness of finance issues, the need to develop skills and enable companies to gain access to strategic market information.

● There is a need to increase dialogue between certain sectors and the finance community in order to address issues relating to the supply and demand of appropriate finance.

Case studies

The following three case studies present the results of a series of seminars held at IPPR aimed at exploring barriers to growth in different industries. They were meant to be brainstorming meetings, bringing together all key players such as small firms, finance and support providers, legal experts, and analysts. The results of the workshops were supplemented by further discussions and meetings.

These case studies are not meant to be comprehensive reports of all the issues facing small firms within each industry. Rather, they are meant to give a flavour of the current concerns of businesspeople and how such issues might be dealt with.

The results of the first seminar on the music industry have already been of use to the Department of Culture Media and Sport who used the paper as a preliminary working paper for a working group on barriers to growth in the music industry. The group brought together all the key trade associations in order to work through and prioritise key areas for future action.

The research makes the points made in the previous chapter very clear. There is no one way to engage particularly the smallest firms in seeking advice and support. Finance issues are specific to sectors and require further detailed discussions between the industry and finance providers. Comprehensive networks of information are needed in most sectors in order to bring together all the disparate support, identify gaps and allow owner-managers to easily find what they need and create opportunities for networks to form to tackle particular issues. Government (whether at the national, regional or local level) has a clear role as a catalyst to encourage all the relevant players to come together to identify issues and propose solutions. The emphasis in all three examples is very much on self-help not top-down generic solutions.

Case Study 1: Management consultancy

Overview of the sector and the role of small firms

Management consultancy is both a mature and a dynamic industry. The UK has the third largest market after the US and Germany, accounting for £5-£6 billion and one billion pounds in exports. Growth rates have been large – 1998 saw an increase in revenues of about 30 per cent[9]. It is an industry which impacts on other sectors, enabling the spread of management best practice and technology transfer.

Management consultancy is defined by the Institute of Management Consultancy as:

> An independent and qualified person who provides a professional service to business, the public and other undertakings by:
>
> ● identifying and investigating problems concerned with strategy, policy, markets, organisations, procedures and methods;
>
> ● formulating recommendations for appropriate action by factual investigation and analysis, with due regard for broader management and business implications;
>
> ● discussing and agreeing with the client the most appropriate course of action;
>
> ● providing assistance where required by the client to implement these recommendations.

Activities include corporate strategy, IT (strategic and systems development/integration), human resources, manufacturing (operations), financial, marketing and project management. Market segments split into strategy, generalist and IT (hardware and software). It is hard, however, to strictly define the sector since companies from outside the industry are increasingly offering consultancy services.

Melvyn Ingleson, from KPMG, offered a new definition of the sector to cope with its changing role – that of 'the exchange of professional knowledge for an agreed reward'. This definition is purposely broad to encompass the drive towards the provision of end-to-end solutions, a trend which is client driven. KPMG has actually dropped the word 'management' from its consultancy services so that it can provide these total solutions. With the increasing spread of management information and use of knowledge management, there is also a move away from providing information to facilitating change within companies.

The industry is currently dominated in the UK by five companies. About 65 per cent of the UK industry is accounted for by companies with over 15 employees and the rest of the industry consists of practices with under 15 consultants and sole practitioners. 55 per cent of consultants work in small companies or by themselves. There seems to have been increasing polarisation between multinationals and smaller companies with both tending to operate in different markets. It appears that mergers and acquisitions have led to a decrease in the number of medium-sized firms and forced smaller companies to focus more on niche markets (Reynolds & Associates, 1993).

Growth within the sector is driven by a variety of factors – gross fixed capital formation, growth or decline of GDP, government expenditure, the development of new consultancy techniques, privatisation of industries – but much is self-generated by new developments in particular fields which spread throughout the industry.

The sector is extremely flexible with freelance consultants working by themselves or with small or larger companies. There is a lot of partnership between companies and between networks of individual consultants or small practices who share work between them. Indeed, the sector exemplifies the 'knowledge worker' – able to work with few capital assets and hence where the size of the firm is not necessarily as important as for other sectors where there are strong economies of scale. At the smaller end of the market there are a variety of business structures ranging from small core companies with hundreds of associates to purely virtual networks, practices who have equity in clients. All of these models reflect different ways to access and retain market share.

Growth at the small end of the market is not really about profitability or sales growth but rather about maximising fee income for individuals thus reflecting the fact that the industry is characterised by the exploitation of knowledge embodied in people. The goal for many small consultancies is not really to become large in terms of employees since fee income can be maximised by working with the flexibility of a market where consultants can join together on different projects. These models of growth illustrate the point made in Chapter 1 that growth can come from the proliferation of smaller competitive companies and the networks between them just as much as from the growth of individual companies.

Smaller companies do, however, face some challenges. A report by Reynolds Associates (1993) pointed out that a SWOT analysis of smaller companies sees strengths arising from WYSIWIG (What You See Is What You Get), greater understanding of SMEs, specialist expertise, and competitive fees. But weaknesses arise from a narrower knowledge and skill base, time management problems, uncertain cashflow, and organisational limitations to meet client needs. However, clients increasingly seem to want specialist expertise – a key driver of growth in the small practice sector.

The industry is represented by the professional body, the Institute of Management Consultancy (IMC), and the trade association, the Management Consultancies Association (MCA). MCA represents consultancies with over 15 employees and the IMC's membership consists of individuals and practices of all sizes.

Growth issues for the industry

- It was suggested that a key factor preventing the growth of the industry as a whole was lack of human capital, not opportunities from clients, and that there is a lack of ability to recruit good people.

- The profile of the sector itself was a cause for concern. It was felt that the sector had an image of being overpriced, not relevant to smaller companies, and was tarnished with certain preconceived and sometimes negative views of consultants' behaviour.

- The trade bodies could potentially do more to promote the image of the industry. At present there is some activity such as the MCA's award for the best case study which is then promoted through the press.

Business models and networks

- The importance of self-employment and networks to the industry was made very clear. The Richmond Group is an example of a virtual network comprised of small practices and individuals.

> The Richmond Group is not new. It was founded 20 years ago. Its 100 members, all of whom are experienced consultants and IMC members, are there to manage opportunity and risk together to support their professional development and the ability to access commercial opportunities. The group meets 6 times a years. They are extremely successful in finding and sharing work. Every week leads or invitations to collaborate are circulated on e-mail. Other activity arises from shared workflows that come from relationships between members which grow through time. The success of this model comes from the ability to form specialist teams for different clients. A lead practice manager manages quality and liases with the client. Technology is not the glue for the network, rather it is strong personal relationships between members, and the ability to share knowledge and work together to win and deliver business.

- It was felt that the main way to tackle issues facing smaller companies is through self-help. One example proposed is that the trade associations and networks could become more like knowledge sharing communities using intranets to promote best practice and benchmarking. Another idea might be to develop more international virtual networks to access foreign markets. This approach could use the equivalent of the IMC in other countries as a focus for bringing potential partners together.

Self-employment

- Concern was expressed at the impact of recent legislation on the flexibility of the market and on freelance consultancy. There was a great deal of hostility to the proposed IR35 (see Chapter Four). It was felt that the industry works well because it is so flexible and that the government's view of the service industries is very out of date. Many argued that if they had to take on freelancers as salaried employees then they would have to raise fees in order to cover peaks and troughs in their activity.

Finance

- Finance is not really an issue for the sector since there are so few start-up costs or fixed assets. The only time that access to finance may be important is if certain intellectual property is commodified into off-the-shelf solutions which could be sold.

Management capabilities and skills

- There seem to be few skill gaps. However, a key issue raised was the lack of marketing capacity which could potentially be a factor holding back further growth. Most people felt that this was a skill preference rather than a skill gap. Many consultants do not want to sell themselves. Some small practices take on marketing executives to sell their services. Another approach adopted is for networks to utilise the services of members who have particular skills and expertise in marketing. This illustrates two models of growth going on side by side – internalising core skills to the company or gaining them through networks.

- There also seems to be a need to increase the spread of best practice, to benchmark, and to commit to more continuous professional development, and to more graduate training.

Industry standards and accreditation

- It was argued that changes in the industry and the degree of mobility of individuals between large and small companies and as freelancers requires the development of widely accepted standards such as the Certified Management Consultant (CMC) professional standard. There was a debate about whether these should be mandatory but all were agreed that there was a need for a basic measure of proficiency. It was also felt that practices themselves needed to be recognised for example as IMC Certified Practices. The general consensus was that this provided a framework, particularly for Government, to give preference to such companies and individuals.

Government's role

- Although most consultants felt that they should tackle most issues themselves, government potentially has a variety of roles in addressing barriers to growth. For example, with regard to the spread of best practice and procurement, the MCA, IMC and HM Treasury have jointly drawn up a statement of best practice which sets out relationships between the client and the consultant.

- There is also a government role in promoting the industry to a wider market. At the meeting it was suggested that it might be possible for the DTI to promote the role of consultants to small firms through, for example, Business Link outlets. One approach would be along similar lines to a recent initiative designed to promote marketing services. Consultation is now going ahead between the government and the IMC on this proposition.

- Additionally 'The sector and policy divisions within the DTI (and presumably other sponsoring departments) are very well-placed to identify competitiveness gaps in industries and sectors of the economy which need a professional consultancy contribution.' (Reynolds & Associates, 1993)

- Management consultancies seem to make little use of Business Links. However, this sector does highlight the fact that the future Small Business Service needs to pay more attention to the needs of self-employed and the models of networked growth outlined above, and to consider in what ways they might be able to support their development.

Case Study 2: Music

The structure of the industry

The UK music industry accounted for £3.2 billion added value in 1997-98 and gross overseas earnings of £1.3 billion (£519 million net)[10]. It is made up of a variety of subsectors including:

- Composition of musical works and music publishing

- Production, retailing and distribution of musical instruments

- Promotion, management and agency-related activities

- Live performance

- Recording and manufacture

- Retailing and distribution of recordings

- Education and training

The recent Creative Industries Taskforce mapping document noted that the industry has been experiencing strong growth in sales over the last decade with the UK being the fourth largest world market for recorded music and even more important as a provider of repertoire. The report also noted that rapid growth could be achieved in the industry, even if UK demand grew moderately, since there is more potential to export to new markets abroad. However, over the last few years export volume has been falling partly due to the strength of the pound and partly to growing sales of indigenous music abroad.

Small firms are widely acknowledged as the creative hotbed of the industry. There are opportunities for some SMEs to grow very fast and some may attempt to do so too quickly. At the same time there are low barriers to entry which means that many people can start out in business ill-prepared. Indeed, the Creative Industries Taskforce noted that much of the dynamism in the sector comes from the smaller end of the market and that there was a need to support UK exports from these companies, and to ensure that they have access to adequate and appropriate business guidance and support.

The high market share of larger companies means that they are able to dictate terms of trade.

Consolidation of the industry has increased the problems for small companies in retail, recording and publishing, for example, in access to retail outlets and promotional tools such as the charts. A major concern of the small independent record companies is that the level of discounting in retail is such that some independent retail stores find it cheaper to buy from chainstores than directly from record companies. They also felt that a key barrier is the high cost of marketing, particularly to enter the singles charts.

The future industry structure and nature of business models is likely to change rapidly with the impact of new technologies. These issues will be dealt with in a forthcoming IPPR publication by Paul Brindley, *New Musical Entrepreneurs*.

At present it is unclear to what extent changes in the market, resulting from say increased access to music via the Internet, will enable smaller companies to get round some of the current barriers to trade arising from the market dominance of the larger companies. Internet and on-line sales, for example, could change current seasonal cashflow, and opportunities for niche markets or new entrants. There are also opportunities for collaboration between companies to create joint promotional opportunities or to use new media and other innovative marketing tools to create and exploit alternative distribution channels. In other words, some of the currently perceived barriers may not be so in the future or they may be very different.

Statistics

- There is a need for improved statistics and a greater understanding of the make-up and dynamics of the sector and its links with other industries. The current government statistics are insufficient for a comprehensive view of the sector and its subsectors. Andy Feist, when presenting the preliminary results of the National Music Council and KPMG 1999 report *A Sound Performance: The economic value of music to the United Kingdom* made the comment that 'if you are unable to identify the industry, then you cannot shout about it'.

- Although the headline performance statistics for the industry indicate that the sector is performing well, there is concern that these broad statistics mask the details of a very complex sector in which certain areas will be doing well while others less so.

Access to finance

- Access to finance seems to be particularly problematic for the industry. (The larger companies have been historically the industry's corporate backers but recently this activity has reduced.) Partly this situation arises from the finance community's lack of understanding and its perception of the music industry. Equally it appears that many music industry business owners are not financially sophisticated. There seems to be a particular problem with demand and supply for equity whether that is for formal or informal venture capital or other more hybrid financing instruments.

Loan finance

- For many small music companies, as for many other SMEs, lack of collateral can be a major problem. For recording companies and publishers, particularly, much of the value of the company will be tied up in intangibles rather than physical assets. Securitisation on the back of intellectual property can be difficult but there are increasing examples of where this has happened although only at the top level of the industry. More generally, however, most music company owners felt that the banks did not understand their specific industry (for example, the seasonal nature of cashflow) or were unable to evaluate it effectively.

- There are, however, some clear exceptions. For example, the following banks are known to specialise in the music industry – Coutts, Barclays SOHO, Natwest Charing Cross, Barclays Broadgate. But this concentration of expertise means that people who approach other banks, particularly outside London, may have difficulties in raising bank finance. However, banks as a whole are increasingly becoming more sophisticated about segmenting their markets along sectoral lines.

- How can banks share sectoral information between branches on the music industry? There needs to be further discussion about ways in which people who go to banks which do not have specific sectoral expertise might be appropriately assessed. It might be that they could be referred on or that the bank manager could access appropriate sector information. A conversation with the

NatWest indicated that their market knowledge has increased markedly although there are some difficulties in spreading information between branches because of issues about data privacy.

- Music industry owners need to understand the banks. The music industry is generally high risk and low return. There are low barriers to entry and hence relatively unskilled and/or rogue businesspeople can enter the market quite easily. Also, music is subject to the vagaries of fashion and bad publicity or to the break up of a band. Future revenue flows can therefore be very uncertain.

- One bank raised the problem that the complexity of the paperwork used by record companies adds to the due diligence costs. The industry appears to use extremely long contracts. It should be quite straightforward to encourage dialogue between the legal profession, banks and music industry to adopt more streamlined contract procedures. The Association of Independent Music (AIM)[11] is looking to produce standard contracts which could be adopted.

- There is a difficulty over the ownership of copyright and assets in the case of bankruptcy. Any bank needs to know that it can recover its debts in the event of a company failing. The problem with many music publishing contracts, for example, is that there is a reversion clause which states that in the event of bankruptcy, the ownership of copyright reverts to the originator, in other words, the writer. The bank is then unable to realise the value of the copyright and hence of the main assets of the company.

- There appears to be little use of the Small Firm Loan Guarantee Scheme within the music industry. Given that the scheme is designed for companies with little collateral, it is surprising that this facility is not made more use of in relation to music companies.

Equity

- With regards to equity, the situation appears to be improving although it is probable that much music industry equity is US-based. It seems that in the US (and increasingly in the UK) there does not seem to be any shortage of equity behind some new internet-based music companies. Derlacher is an example of a finance broker that leverages loan and equity finance into packages specifically for businesses in music and other industries specialising in new media content and applications.

- It was felt that there was a need to encourage the formation of more specialist venture capitalist funds or brokers or to develop more appropriate finance instruments for example mezzanine or patient loans. The US seems to have many more specialised funds than the UK. Specialist expertise in funds can help finance providers seek out appropriate firms to support and may also be more acceptable to companies because they understand their industry.

- There is a need to increase understanding amongst owner-managers about the benefits and relevance of the use of equity.

- Sectoral business angel networks might help to encourage more people to provide equity whether individually or through syndicates where one or more angels may have expertise in the industry. An added advantage of this approach is that it might well encourage industry professionals to put something back into the industry and provide help and expertise to the owner managers. This approach could be linked to the National Business Angels Network or linked to music industry information networks.

- The film industry has been quite innovative about encouraging a wide range of people to support new ventures through, for example, equity that allows people to take part as an extra in film. Maybe there are ways of encouraging small investors in the music industry through inventive schemes, particularly at local level. An important aspect of this type of approach is that it encourages people that would not normally invest to do so and also helps to fund more risky ventures where the return might be lower than that generally required by a business angel.

Increasing financial awareness

- Increased financial literacy could be encouraged through including financial and business issues in entry-level vocational courses. There is a potential parallel with an initiative undertaken by the NatWest together with the fashion industry, which encourages training courses for entrants to the industry to include financial and business skills. There could be increased dialogue with Metier to see where such skills can be included into as many vocational training courses as possible. However, a problem here is that many people in the music industry will not undergo formal training and so this route may well have limited impact.

- There needs to be increased provision and availability of advice and support on finance to owner-managers through a variety of channels. This is dealt with under advice and support below.

Applicability of government incentive schemes

- As noted at the beginning of this chapter, the Enterprise Investment Scheme is not applicable to many music companies because a proportion of their income comes from royalties. A new government incentive scheme – the Enterprise Management Incentive – aimed at encouraging high flying managers to leave big business and work with dynamic smaller companies, is also not applicable to some companies in the music industry for the same reasons.

Business advice and support

- As indicated above, it is generally believed that there is a lack of business skills amongst many owner-managers in the music industry. Many people have training in music-related skills and have a high technological awareness but do not possess all the skills necessary to set up and run a business.

- Many business owners have no idea of all the available government support. There is quite clearly a need for increased marketing of government schemes to the sector, the creation of a variety of access points and more signposting. There are already many channels which could be used to spread information, for example, trade associations, music press, banks, development agencies – but it will be important to ensure that the multiplicity of information does not add to confusion but creates a comprehensive network.

- It appears that most music industry owner-managers had either never heard of Business Links or did not think that they provided appropriate support. Although it was acknowledged that generic skills were important, it was felt that these should be passed on by industry professionals and in groups where other businesspeople came from the same sector or similar industries.

- There are examples of music or creative industry development agencies and other specific provision:

> Merseyside Music Development Agency (funded predominantly by Objective 1 European money) aims to 'improve the provision of business support and financial assistance for music industry start-ups, indigenous expansion and inward investment.' There is a Music Enterprise Service which provides advice and support, a comprehensive website with an on-line music industry directory and newsletters. This agency behaves like a local trade association by doing research, educating financiers and looking at training needs.

> In Sheffield, an integrated approach to both regeneration and business support has resulted in the formation of a creative industries cluster with workspaces, access to specialised advice and support and the creation of a collaborative culture of sharing resources and skills between companies. A key element to this approach is the creation of sustainable public-private partnerships drawing on existing business support services and the local finance community.

> Manchester Technology Management Centres employ associates and consultants to deliver SME support with City Council support and European funds. One centre specialises in the creative industries. There is also a North West New Media Network driven by demand to fill the gap for industry specific business services. The driver behind these initiatives is that every business owner needs a backbone of news and industry intelligence to inform decision-making. There is also a move to develop internet portals which can access a range of information and to investigate the role of learning through online business task wizards.

- It is very important to reach as many people as possible who have no current access to sector advice and support. Not everyone will be close to a local development agency or sectoral expertise. Clearly there is great scope here for the use of on-line networks and services. It should also be possible to create a situation where all banks, enterprise agencies, Business Links and Local Authorities should have access to appropriate information that at the very least enables them to signpost people on to appropriate providers and services. It might be possible to work with banks and accountants to provide, for example, tailored financial information to music industry companies through leaflets, on-line advice or via half-day briefings.

- One useful DCMS/DTI/Trade Association initiative could be to create and pump-prime an industry-run single access point website which could incorporate information on government schemes, signpost on to on-line or local expertise and act as a focal point for bringing together disparate initiatives. It could also link to the University for Industry and provide innovative online delivery of business support as and when needed. This would be particularly helpful for those people who have no time to undergo more formal training or who cannot access appropriate resources in their locality. The network could also act to encourage more collaboration between companies along the lines of the Merseyside Music Export Consortium mentioned in Chapter Four. It could also provide a platform for finance providers to match and access suitable funding opportunities in a similar way to the Software Business Network. The DCMS and the trade associations are currently considering the potential of such an initiative.

Role of the trade associations

- Trade associations should be ideal ways to pass information on about available government schemes, relevant training and also provide their own training. A danger is that there will be duplication and fragmentation of support so there needs to be careful mapping of current and potential activity with a view to sharing expertise and linking up to other sources of advice and training. In a recent meeting held at DCMS, the trade associations for the industry were keen to come together to pool resources.

Building on networks

- As noted above, one of the ways in which small companies can get over the problems of lack of market power is to join together. It seems that, although there is a great deal of networking between individuals in the industry, there is less so between businesses. The International Managers Forum is one example of a peer group that swaps expertise but there could well be room for many more innovative networking initiatives whether at local, regional or national level. These networks can act as focal points for swapping information about future developments, government information, accessing finance or for providing the base for more formal links between companies through, say, joint marketing initiatives. Or they could be used for simple things such as accessing good accountants with experience of the industry. These groups could be catalysed by local development agencies or trade associations. There could also be more development of virtual networking opportunities for those who are not physically close to other people within the industry.

Mentors

- AIM is setting up a scheme whereby established businesspeople within the industry can pass on knowledge to up and coming record companies. This kind of approach could be extended throughout the industry. Encouraging mentors is also similar to encouraging experienced business people to become business angels. Both strategies attempt to harness business expertise and specific sectoral expertise as well as to create a situation whereby successful people are able to put something back into the industry.

Access to export markets and trading overseas

- Accessing foreign markets involves substantial resources. Many small music publishers often license/subpublish through companies with large market share and significant bargaining and purchasing power. Some record companies have opened their own offices in key territories and found that this appears to be a good way to develop overseas markets.

- There is poor understanding of what government can offer, for example, in trade missions. It was felt that trade missions seem to be more geared to the needs of manufacturing companies than other industries.

- Many business-owners are unaware of the needs of foreign markets or the ways of dealing with issues such as withholding tax, or the repatriation of performance income.

- Few people are aware of the ways of avoiding withholding tax. In some territories however it is unavoidable. This tax is embedded in tax treaties but there is a question over why it should exist at all. One accountant suggested that the ideal situation would be that you are paid gross and are assessed by the recipient country tax authority. There seems to be little argument for its continuation in Europe.

Case Study 3: Printing

Overview of the industry

The UK print industry accounts for 1.7 per cent of GDP – £12.8 billion. It comprises 12,000 companies, employs 170,000 people directly and is growing at a rate of two per cent per year reflecting the general nature of the economy). The industry is geographically dispersed – there are printers everywhere – and there are no major concentrations anywhere in the UK although there are some small clusters, for example, in London. The industry is dominated by very small companies – 90 per cent employ less than 20 people and there are only 20 companies with over 400 employees. The firms are predominantly owner-managed. The industry is extremely fragmented in every sense – geographically, market sector, product type.[12]

Printing is highly competitive with excess capacity in the industry and price-cutting which makes it hard for smaller firms to compete with the larger companies. Smaller firms can best compete by offering niche services but many printers at the bottom end of the market are jobbing printers who offer general services.

The extent of the different print markets is set out below:

Market	Share %	Comment
Newspapers	23	largest companies, medium trading margin
Magazines and catalogues	13	medium margins
Commercial print	10	low margins, extremely fragmented
Direct mail	10	higher margins
Books	5	lower margins
Security print	3	higher margins
Other	33	very fragmented, low margins

The overriding driver of change in the industry is currently digitialisation. It is affecting all three key stages of the printing process: – pre-press where data is prepared ready to print (traditionally 'paste-up'); press – printing the ink onto paper (traditionally litho, gravure or screen); and, to a lesser extent, producing the final product. Although these technology changes mean that printing may be sourced anywhere in the world, there is evidence that this process may be reversing as other factors than low cost become important, such as providing total and customised services (CEEDR, 1997).

The implications are that:

- Staff will have to become fully computer literate, and able to work with advanced networks and storage equipment, as well as understanding the older technology. Labour flexibility will be critical.

- Greater customer-facing skills are required as customers can now provide their digital data directly.

- General management skills are becoming essential as, what was often done outside (due to its complexity), is now done in-house.

- Entry barriers are reduced so that competition can come from elsewhere, particularly outside of traditional printing and from overseas.

- Most 'capital' assets are now computers where lifetime is determined by chip power.

- Customers are demanding and receiving faster turnaround and more control. They will increasingly demand shorter runs, variable data usage and short notice changes.

- There is less waste and pollution from chemical processes.

- There are major opportunities for printers to evolve into print-service organisations, and into data management businesses, for example managing and publishing customer's data on paper, on the internet, or on CD ROM.

Other drivers are changing customer demands (the demand for, and availability of, information, both in business and in the home) and the impact of environmental concerns.

The printing industry is evolving from a craft-based business to an automated information service business. The role of print as a separate entity from 'communications' is decreasing. Printing is therefore becoming a smaller slice of a much larger cake. But as Averil Hopkins pointed out in the seminar:

The future of print is very bright – if the industry can survive the economic problems resulting from the technical changes underway and to come, and if printers can evolve from ink-on-paper craftsmen to information service managers.

Impact of digitalisation

- It was felt that digitalisation would not develop linearly – it will suddenly take-off. No-one really knows the exact pace of change and it is hard for the industry to make those judgements. What it does mean, however, is that firms will have to keep up-to-date and ensure that employees have the skills to cope with change.

- The impact of digitalisation is probably going to be worse for very small companies who will find it hard to invest in the new equipment and software.

- There have always been tax breaks on fixed assets. As the industry (and many others) move to a less asset-based infrastructure, there is more of an argument for providing relief for funds left within a business especially where there are competing pressures on profits, for example, to put into pensions.

- What is a high-tech business? Printing is seen as low-tech but is increasingly using extremely high-tech machinery. The recent Competitiveness White Paper (DTI, 1998) defines high-tech industries in a very particular way and has focused support there. Another problem is that the perception of the industry is low-tech and 'messy' which appears to make it unattractive to younger people.

Interlinkages within the industry

- There is a likelihood of further consolidation and convergence in the industry but at present there is not that much evidence of mergers and acquisitions. There are strong patterns of inter-linkages between firms but these are changing with technological change. There is more likelihood of collaboration through sharing work and providing complimentary services. Some of this activity happens already but it was felt that there was probably not enough.

- Clustering and networking allow smaller firms to compete with larger companies. However, although CEEDR (1997) found examples of clusters, they were very dependent on different sub-sectors and there was great variety in the extent to which printers themselves recognised the existence of the cluster. The authors thought that policy should be wary of trying to create collaborative activities between firms partly because many printers are concerned about working with competitors. They believed however that it might be possible to encourage joint training or recruitment activities within local networks.

- Most alliances are built up through word of mouth but it was felt that you need to trust the other partners. However, many people believed that printers will have to become able to work with others if they are to create the alliances needed in the future.

- It was suggested that the British Printing Industries Federation (BPIF) could be a way to create more links between companies but membership of the trade association does not guarantee trustworthiness or quality. Another problem that the membership of the BPIF does not include the smallest companies. However, it does link up with other parts of the industry and could build on these contacts.

Finance

- Printing is a highly competitive and high-risk industry and the banks are very aware of this. There is a low expectation of long-run profit but there are some sub-sectors with lower competition and higher profit margins (CEEDR, 1997).

- There seems to be a tendency towards over-investment in an industry where firms are driven by the need to obtain the latest equipment. 'A lack of business planning and inadequate investment appraisal in many smaller firms can lead to investment in equipment that may not be cost effective.' (CEEDR, 1997)

- There seems to be a low level of financial expertise amongst smaller printing owner-managers. 56 per cent of managers in a recent survey for the BPIF (Smallbone *et al*, 1997) recognised the need for financial management advice and sources of finance. There also seems to be an absence of growth planning in the industry and a lot of short-termism.

- In order to tackle the lack of financial literacy, it was suggested that it might be possible to include finance skills within entry-level training to the industry. But this still leaves the question of how to increase the financial expertise of existing companies. The networks mentioned below might help in this respect.

- It was felt that banks could encourage the use of asset finance or invoice discounting more within the industry. This is a very appropriate form of finance for a sector with late payment periods and unstable income.

- It was felt that the banks have other roles, for example, in reviewing debtor books and hence encouraging businesspeople to look at their creditors more carefully and to consider alternative forms of finance. The banks might perhaps become more proactive in this approach in order to encourage a change of culture.

- For specialist equipment, it is possible to use specific finance companies or hire purchase. However, as equipment becomes more high tech, this can become increasingly difficult since the value of the product will depreciate extremely fast.

- There seems to be little opportunity for business angel finance in the sector since there tend to be low returns. However, there are examples of its use in those companies that are creating new approaches to delivering printing solutions. There could be dialogue between the BPIF and the new National Business Angel Network to discuss how to increase awareness of business angels within the industry and perhaps create the possibility of specific sector matching.

Workforce skills

- Both small and medium-sized companies complain about skill shortages. It is apparently hard to find multi-skilled people.

- There is likely to be a shift away from employing 16-year-old apprentices to recruiting 18-year-olds who can learn more effectively. All future employees will have to be multi-skilled and forward looking.

- It is problematic to train in a small company because it is very difficult to find time to leave the business premises. The erratic nature of the business also means that it is difficult to plan to attend training sessions at set times. Recent research with the industry resulted in demand for training which was not in work hours and at no cost! Experience indicates that evening or morning courses are the best approach.

- A critical problem is that although some companies do invest in training their workforce, others will just poach trained staff.

- A voluntary training levy has some attraction for the industry in terms of funding the National Training Organisation (NTO) more adequately but it was felt that the industry would not accept this.

- New ways to train will have to be found since the number of colleges offering training has dropped. It was believed that 10 years ago there was a perception in Europe that the UK had the best training infrastructure but this situation is no longer the case since there has been a gradual withdrawal of funding.

Advice and support for owner managers

- There are general management and finance skills gaps, particularly for existing firms. Entrant firms tend to have a broader mix of skills from outside the industry. Surveys have highlighted the kinds of management needs in the industry (CEEDR, 1997; Smallbone *et al*, 1997) such as marketing, business planning, customer relations, recruitment, impartial advice on equipment. A primary need is to understand the impact of change on firms and then advice and consultancy to help companies adapt. The reports also made the point that this demand for support was by those who recognised their inadequacies but that there was also a need for diagnostic services for those firms, particularly the smallest, to increase their understanding of what they might need.

- CEEDR (1997) concluded that there was a latent demand for business support but that printers were being frustrated by the plethora of providers. They reported a need to increase ease of access to services by networking support providers together (for example, trade associations, TECs, Links, enterprise agencies) in order to reduce confusion and increase the total market for advice. They felt that, although generic advice might be appropriate, many printers preferred advisors to have expertise in their field. It is this perception that matters when trying to encourage increased take-up of advice and support. They suggested a role for local sector specific training and the creation of forums at a subregional level which bring together all support and finance providers to network resources and find solutions to problems.

- There is a tension between the impression that most owner-managers will not talk to anyone who does not come from the industry and the perception that the best managers come from outside the industry. The industry is changing away from being a craft and new management and entrepreneurship skills are needed.

- It was felt that TECs do not seem to have provided much specific support for the industry because printing is not geographically concentrated. However, they could have a role in providing information on advice, support and training, to printers in their area.

In order to reach the smallest companies and those who probably need the most help, a variety of approaches could be used:

- Build on the presence of a higher education facility to provide benchmarking and spread best practice amongst local firms.

- Develop local area clusters to share problems and work (bearing in mind the difficulties mentioned above). It was felt that networks should be peer groups and not initiated by government. A key question arises as to who the catalyst would be for these networks. It was suggested that members of the BPIF could be catalysts for this kind of activity in an area. Banks and accountants could also be pivotal in encouraging people to become involved and perhaps might host some of the networks.

- Smallbone *et al* (1997) suggested that the BPIF could take on a proactive role to promote mentors for small companies and encourage them to take up diagnostic services to identify their needs. The participants in the seminar felt that mentoring is an excellent way to support managers. Mentoring is often through the appointment of Non-Executive Directors who can act as a counter-balance to the very family-oriented nature of most print-based businesses.

- There was a feeling that it might be possible to use new technologies to support learning by owner-managers and provide flexibility in access to advice. IT solutions could be used for example, for service provision, case studies, benchmarking, or best practice.

Regional Innovation Strategy (RIS) in West Yorkshire

The regional policy role was determined to be to identify and recognise barriers to innovation, exploit partnerships between academia and industry and spread best practice. The key aims are to facilitate the adaptation of the industry to change, develop a regional knowledge network, provide incubation for new ideas and increase regional access to skills. There will be a distributed Centre of Excellence for Print and Packaging Technology, a pool of graduate expertise from Leeds Metropolitan University, and a centralised programme to raise awareness of available schemes in order to avoid duplication between support providers and to identify new needs. The RIS is also linking up with the White Rose Faraday Centre for Enhanced Packaging Technology. There will also be a one-stop internet facility which will, for example, profile best practice and audit services.

- The Government has been addressing the sectoral dimension of management training to some extent. For example, managing technology programmes have been set up for printing. The new RDAs are also addressing sectoral issues. A regional innovation strategy for printing has already been developed in West Yorkshire and this may be rolled out around the country. Such an approach may answer part of the problem of reaching the many small printing companies and could be used as the start of more comprehensive initiatives.

- There was a concern that not enough money is being targeted on sectors, rather it is flowing through to Business Links or to the regions.

- It was felt that there is a lot of duplication of research into the needs of the print industry and not enough development of the results of that research into positive responses. However, even when they are, there may be a lack of collaboration between service providers. For example, the regional strategies were begun without talking to the trade association.

- It was clear from the discussions that there is no one body that can fill the skill and management gaps. There needs to be a whole range of inputs and approaches, for example, the BPIF, hardware suppliers who provide training, local networks, further education colleges, print and electronic media, Business Links and enterprise agencies. This underpins the point made by CEEDR of the need to pool resources and network providers together. This will be important at the local, regional and national level in order to tackle issues such as encouraging more micro-enterprises to take up support or to address more general finance issues with private sector providers. This is an area where the RDAs, the future Small Business Service and the BPIF should all be involved in creating the appropriate infrastructure. Such activity will require very flexible funding. But if CEEDR is right, the sectoral approach could be the way to increase the demand for business support and increase the engagement of the smallest printing companies.

Bibliography

Aston University Business School (1990) *Constraints on the Growth of Small Firms* A report of a survey of small firms by Aston Business School.

Audretsch D *et al* (1998) *Are Small Firms Really Sub-optimal?* EIM Research Report, Zoetermeer, The Netherlands.

Barkham R, Gudgin G, Hart M, Hanvey E (1996) *The determinants of small firm growth* Jessica Kingsley, London.

Bennett R and Robson P (1999) *Business Link: service use, satisfaction and comparison with Business Shop and Business Connect* mimeo, Department of Geography, University of Cambridge.

Bradburd and Ross (1989) 'Can small firms find and defend strategic niches? A test of the Porter hypothesis' *Review of Economics and Statistics* Vol LXXI, May, No 2, pp 258-62.

Brindley P (forthcoming) *New Musical Entrepreneurs: driving innovation in the digital economy* IPPR.

Bryson J R (1997) 'Business Link and the New Knowledge Workers', *Policy Studies* Vol 18, No 1, 67-80

Cambridge Small Business Research Centre (1992) *The State of British Enterprise* Department of Applied Economics, Cambridge.

Carroll R, Holtz-Eakin D, Rider M, Rosen H S (1996) *Income Taxes and Entrepreneurs' Use of Labour* Centre for Economic Policy Studies Working Paper, No 32, July, US.

Castells M (1995) *The new business world: Networks and firms* discussion paper for the ILO Enterprise Forum 96, Panel 2(a).

CBI (1997) *Tech Stars: Breaking the growth barriers for technology-based SMEs*.

CEC (1999) *White Paper on Commerce,* Communication from the Commission COM (99) 6 Final.

CEEDR (1997) *Report on the Paper, Printing and Publishing Sector Study in London and the Lee Valley* Centre for Enterprise and Economic Development Research, University of Middlesex, Commissioned for NLTEC, LETEC and SOLOTEC.

Cressy R and Storey D (1995) *New Firms and Their Bank* NatWest Bank, London.

Curran J, Berney R, Jari K (1999) *A Critical Evaluation of Industry SME Support Policies in the United Kingdom and the Republic of Ireland* Stage One Report, An In-Depth Delphi Study of Selected SME

Support Policies and Their Evaluation, Ministry of Trade and Industry, Finland, Studies and Reports, 5/1999.

DTI (1998) *Our Competitive Future – Building the Knowledge-Driven Economy* DTI.

DTI (1999a) *The Small Business Service: A Public Consultation* URN 99/815, DTI.

DTI (1999b) *Small and Medium Enterprise (SME) Statistics for the United Kingdom 1998* SME Statistics Unit, DTI, August 1999, Government Statistical Service, URN 99/92.

Ernst and Young (1996) *Evaluation of Business Links*.

European Commission (1998) *Enterprises in Europe* Fifth Report, SME Project, Eurostat.

Evans D S (1987) 'Tests of Alternative Theories of Firm Growth' in *Journal of Political Economy* 95, 657-674.

Folster S (1999) *Do entrepreneurs create jobs?* The Swedish Research Institute of Trade, Stockholm, Sweden.

Gallagher C and Botham R (1998) *New Firms and Job Creation in Contrasting Regional Economies: Some Empirical Evidence and Policy Implications* a paper presented to the 28th European Seminar on Small Business Research, Vienna, Sep 98.

Gallagher and Miller (1991) 'New Fast Growing Companies Create Jobs' *Long Range Planning* Vol 24, No 1, pp. 96-101.

Gavron R, Cowling M, Holtham G, and Westall A (1998) *The Entrepreneurial Society* IPPR.

Gray C (1998) *Enterprise and Culture* London, Routledge.

Harding R (1999) *Venture Capital and Regional Development* IPPR.

KPMG (1999) *An Evaluation of the Small Firms Loan Guarantee Scheme*.

NUTEK (1998) *Swedish Industry and Industrial Policy* Swedish National Board for Industrial and Technical Development, Stockholm, Sweden.

OECD (1994) *Employment Outlook*.

OECD (1996) *SMEs: Employment, Innovation and Growth* The Washington Workshop.

OECD (1998a) *High-growth SMEs and Employment: Assessment of best practice policies:* Country Study: France; Preliminary report 'The growth trajectory of high-growth firms' Directorate for Science, Technology and Industry, Industry Committee, DSTI/IND/PME(98)25.

OECD (1998b) *High-growth SMEs and Employment: Assessment of best practice* Highlights of preliminary findings in Phase 1, Statistical analysis: firm growth types, employment and sectoral composition.

Office World (1994) *Office World Quarterly Small Business Survey* Reading.

PACEC (1998) *Business Links – Value for Money Evaluation* Cambridge.

Parker K T and Vickerstaff S (1996) 'TECs, LECs and small firms: differences in provision and performance' *Environment and Planning C*, Vol 14, 251-267.

Penrose E (1959) *The Theory of the Growth of the Firm* Oxford, Basil Blackwell.

Phillips B D and Kirchoff B A (1989) 'Formation, growth and survival; small firm dynamics in the US economy' *Small Business Economics* Vol 1, No1, 65-74.

Priest S J (1999) 'Business Link Services to SMEs: targetting, innovation and charging' *Environment and Planning C* Vol 17, 177-193.

Reid G, Jacobsen L, Andersen M (1993) *Profiles in Small Business: A competitive strategy approach* London, Routledge.

Reid G (1995) 'Early life-cycle behaviour of micro firms in Scotland' in *Small Business Economics* Vol 7, 89-95.

Reynolds & Associates Ltd (1993) *Analysis of the Management Consultancy Sector* prepared for TR Division, DTI, (Ref: EC/4654/93).

Reynolds P (1993) *High Performance Entrepreneurship: What makes it different?* paper presented at Babson Entrepreneurial Conference, University of Houston, 24-7 March.

Reynolds P, Storey D J and Westhead P (1994) 'Cross-national comparisons of the Variation in New Firm Formation Rates' *Regional Studies* 28.4, pp 443-456.

Smallbone D (1995) 'The Characteristics and Strategies of High Growth SMEs' in *International Journal of Entrepreneurial Behaviour and Research* Vol 1, No 3.

Smallbone D, Baldock R, Fadahunsi A (1997) *Researching the Business Support Needs of Firms in the Printing and Packaging Industry* Final Report to the BPIF, Centre for Enterprise and Economic Development Research, Middlesex University.

Smallbone D, Baldock R, and Supri S (1999) *New Technology and Related Skills Needs in the Printing and Publishing Industries* Centre for

Enterprise and Economic Development Research, University of Middlesex.

Storey (1994) *Understanding the Small Business Sector* Routledge, London.

Taylor M P (1996) 'Self-employment in the UK: Earnings, Independence, or Unemployment: Why become self-employed' *Oxford Bulletin of Economics and Statistics* Vol. 58, No. 2, 253-265.

Taylor M P (1997) *Survival of the Fittest? An Analysis of Self-Employment Duration in Britain* ESRC Centre for Micro Social Change, University of Essex.

West M and Patterson M (1999) 'The workforce and productivity' *New Economy* Vol 6, No 1, 22-27, IPPR, Blackwell.

Wylie (1996) *Mergers between TECs and Chambers* Paper presented to conference on Building Better Business Links: Networking for Industry, London.

Endnotes

1. Microenterprises are defined generally as 0-9 employees; small firms, 10-49; medium, 50-249; large, 250+.

2. Data from a conversation with the DTI SME Policy Unit.

3. But note that the sample only represented manufacturing firms.

4. Paul Burns was speaking at a seminar on growth at the Local Economy Policy Unit at the University of the South Bank in June 1999.

5. We know that venture capital backed companies have a higher growth rate and create more jobs, see for example BVCA 'Incentivising management' *Budget Submission 1999/2000.*

6. Following the success of the programmes based at Warwick, the programme has now been rolled out to Milton Keynes where the CSME team has developed a partnership with the local BL supported by the European Social Fund.

7. These comments were made in a paper presented at the Local Economy Policy Unit of the University of South Bank seminar on small business growth in June 99.

8. This analysis was provided by Alison Wenham of AIM in a note to the DCMS on the impact of licensing on record company revenues.

9. This data was provided by MCA for the seminar.

10. Data from the National Music Council and KPMG study: *A Sound Performance: The value of music to the UK economy* 1999.

11. AIM is the trade association for independent record companies which was set up recently to address business issues (generally for smaller companies).

12. The analysis for this sector and the impact of digitalisation was provided by Averil Horton of Alpha to Omega Ltd.